SWEETER
THAN
REVENGE

Sweeter than Revenge

OVERCOMING YOUR PAYBACK MIND

David Richo

SHAMBHALA

Shambhala Publications, Inc.
2129 13th Street
Boulder, Colorado 80302
www.shambhala.com

Cover design: Amanda Weiss
Interior design: Kate Huber-Parker

9 8 7 6 5 4 3 2 1

First Edition
Printed in the United States of America

Shambhala Publications makes every effort
to print on acid-free, recycled paper.
Shambhala Publications is distributed worldwide by
Penguin Random House, Inc., and its subsidiaries.

Library of Congress Cataloging-in-Publication Data
Names: Richo, David, 1940– author
Title: Sweeter than revenge: overcoming your payback mind / David Richo.
Description: First edition. | Boulder, Colorado: Shambhala Publications, [2025]
Identifiers: LCCN 2025005253 | ISBN 9781645474708 trade paperback
Subjects: LCSH: Revenge—Psychological aspects
Classification: LCC BF637.R48 R53 | DDC 152.4/7—dc23/eng/20250521
LC record available at https://lccn.loc.gov/2025005253

The authorized representative in the EU for product safety
and compliance is eucomply OÜ, Pärnu mnt 139b-14, 11317
Tallinn, Estonia, hello@eucompliancepartner.com.

To Joshua, Carolyn, Siena, Nathaniel, Nicholas

May we show all the love we have

in any way we can, wherever we may be,

today and all the time,

to everyone—including ourselves—

since love is what all humans are

and what we're here to share.

May nothing matter to us more than love

or give us greater joy.

May all our world become,

through us, with us, in us:

one Sacred Heart of love.

CONTENTS

PREFACE

At this especially tumultuous and challenging time in our history, I feel a summons to use whatever talent I have as a writer and teacher to explore the violence that is revenge and offer some psychological and spiritual alternatives to it. I appreciate whatever holy spirit entrusted—and trusted—me with this so precious and crucial calling. I am also grateful for feeling an abiding enthusiasm for this calling and for whatever skill I have to fulfill it. I see it as nothing less than an invitation to join in constructing a habitat for humanity.

Revenge is not limited to international events. It can happen in any relationship, even intimate ones. A psychological given of all embracing is that we sometimes scrape one another. We will benefit from a nonviolent plan to meet that eventuality as individuals and nations, especially now that the daily news reports retaliations at all levels. We can find ways to handle the stress those reports batter our bodies with. This book attempts to equip us with the gear required on our steep hike up the scary trail.

We may not be successful at eliminating our impulse to retaliate, but we can stop acting on it. We can tame our vindictive ego's inclinations. The relay of inflicting pain and taking revenge in our interactions can stop with us. Of course it will take enormous effort not to act on our ingrained habit of retaliation. It will take courage and self-compassion not to give up on our practice of nonviolence, though we may often fail in it. It will take an openness to transformation if we are ever to fulfill the splendid requirements of love or even believe that nonretaliation has value.

My hope is that we will someday soon become willing to employ alternatives to retaliation in relationships and in politics. Instead of accepting without protest the standard public policy of avenging, we can root for a spiritual alternative. We can do all we can, publicly or privately, to be emissaries of justice in the face of injustice, of peace in the face of war, of love in the face of hate. Justice does not mean retribution, but restoration of community. Peace does not mean no war happening now, but an international ban on it altogether. Love does not mean only forgiveness of a wrong, but not keeping score of wrongs at all.

The will in us to exact vengeance, which is escalatory by definition, comes down to nothing less than a drive toward death. We know cooperation and peace are how humans can survive but we more often choose the death-row exit strategies of revenge and war. The statement "We have to fight back and protect ourselves, so war is justified" is the same as "There is no alternative to revenge." These statements sound like war and revenge are the only plans we humans can think up. Yet we have ingenuity. We are certainly not myopic; we have gigantic vision. We are not primitive; we are better than that. We are not one-trick ponies; we are virtuosos. We can widen the range of our moral imagination and moral courage. This book is about reclaiming those gifts. Our focus is on a moral, spiritual path to true justice.

These pages do not offer a scientific study of revenge. They assert that nonretaliation is an ethical choice as well as an ingredient of psychological health and spirituality. We hope that our individual commitment to letting go of revenge will serve as a first step to ending it in the world. What follows is a match struck boldly in the dark to see how such a wish can come true.

Finally, I am deeply thankful to my editor at Shambhala, Beth Frankl, who saw an importance and unique value in this book from the very beginning; she graced me with a guiding hand and encouraging heart to its completion. I also appreciate the staff at Shambhala who so skillfully and diligently helped in the birthing of this book. It has meant so much to me to have assisting forces—staff, friends, and holy spirit—join me in my calling to be of some help to individuals and, hopefully, society too. This book, like all books, is indeed the result of team effort. "Teamwork" is ultimately a form of intimacy: the glittering goal and precious prize of all our spiritual practice.

David Richo
San Francisco, October 7, 2023

SWEETER

THAN

REVENGE

INTRODUCTION

I was brought up to believe in revenge as an appropriate and necessary way to handle injury of any kind. I lived in accord with this primitive bias for many years, never questioning my behavior, never naming my own mean-spirited vindictive manner, even in my so-called loving relationships. Vendetta, practiced actively or passively, was just automatic in me, my default setting anytime someone crossed or wronged me in any way. It was not until I had been engaging in spiritual practices *for over twenty years* that I was ready to recognize and let go of my payback style. Yes, it can take that long. As we shall see, this letting go of revenge turns out to be the same as letting go of the illusion of separateness—the true cause of suffering.

This book is an invitation to explore particularly the element of revenge that may creep into intimate relationships, often without being named as such by the partners. Revenge comes from the shadow side of relating, the narcissistic ego side that seeks self-satisfaction rather than effective mutuality. In exacting revenge there are no ties, no attention to mutuality. Even in the ties of family, marriage, relationship, or fellow citizenship, people still retaliate. From the murder of family members to civil wars, we see that vengeful aggression knows no bounds. Not even love makes us safe from the revenge of others, nor are others safe from us.

1

This book proposes a path to healthy and spiritually conscious relationships that is sweeter than revenge: acting with loving-kindness, communicating feelings and responses nonviolently, letting go of ego, and forgiving again and again. In the following chapters we will explore all four of these practices—portals of freedom from the payback mind. We then find ways to choose reconciliation over retribution, forgiveness over payback, compassion over judgment, love over division. Yes, we can find spiritually skillful ways to respond when others hurt us or retaliate against us when we hurt them. They work best when we make a moral commitment to a life of radical oneness instead of having to be the one who is right. That one is of course nothing more than ego. Radical mutuality is the only path out of the ego divisiveness on which revenge so ravenously forages.

Retaliation is often an automatic first response to aggression. When retaliation is a compulsive go-to, we have lost the power of choice, lost our freedom to explore and act on alternatives. This book is about making a choice rather than acting on a reflex. We will explore how this can happen in our personal relationships and on the world stage.

In any case, we keep in mind that the will to get back at someone who hurt us is totally normal, not irrational, not a sign of a psychological illness or an inclination toward immorality.

OLD IN THE PSYCHE

The other day I saw my grandson, Nate, age six, swing his arm and unintentionally hit my other grandson, Nick, age two, who instantly tapped him back, but not in a harming way. I guessed the toddler somehow understood that retaliation is a useful deterrent to further harm. None of us taught him this. Safety through revenge seems built-in to being human—standard equipment, mostly involuntary. We notice in this story also that retaliation is based on perceived injustice. There was no actual aggression, but what happened to Nick *felt like* aggression. So our alternative practice begins with checking out how something happened and what the intention was so we know what is really going on.

Our ancient ancestors probably engaged in revenge to discourage crime and injustice. Even now, if someone knows we will retaliate, they will be more likely to be respectful of our boundaries and rights. When we show that we will seek payback, we warn others to think twice about offending us. Our guaranteed retaliatory style can also protect us from others' preemptive aggression. Our manner displays the flag that warns: "Don't tread on me!" Yet dialogue that leads to reform and reconciliation is a more spiritually conscious option. It works on the basis of cooperation, the enterprise ensuring the triumph of human solidarity. Its flag says: "Let's tread the path together to a solution."

MANY FORMS

Retaliation can take minor or major forms and be shown in active or passive ways. An act of revenge may be cruel, even criminal, like causing physical harm or death. It can even be an atrocity of war. In less severe instances, we retaliate with road rage against someone who cuts us off in traffic. We may be underhanded and covert in how we get back at others or be openly mean. We may immediately react to a provocation with vengeance or bide our time and strike like Zorro. We may refuse to return a phone call because someone did not return ours months ago. We might be openly or indirectly vindictive because we were passed over for a promotion.

Our act of retaliation may be hardly noticeable by us, like not answering a text. Retaliation may also seem quite appropriate. For instance, we invited Mabel to our party but she did not invite us to hers, so we will not invite her to ours anymore. We might even place an advertisement like this humorous one I once saw: "For Sale: One wedding ring, never worn. One gun, fired only once."

DIVISION AND ONENESS

Retaliation thrives on division, which is a contradiction of the fact and necessity of human connectedness, of survival by cooperation. It also flies in the face of Buddhist and other spiritual teachings on oneness and human solidarity. The first truth in Buddhism is that suffering is a given of life. Retaliation in relationships is about passing the suffering of the victim back to the one who caused it. Retaliation is thus not a healing response to suffering but a plan to enact it further. Buddhist practice is about ending suffering; retaliation is about prolonging it.

A spiritual challenge is to accept the fact of oneness, to see and honor the intimacy among all beings. We let go of retaliation when we are no longer caught in the illusion that we are separate selves, each looking out for number one. Then a kindly affinity becomes victorious in our relationships. There is not one Buddhist practice that is consonant with retaliation. We might ask ourselves: Did anything in my upbringing, religion, or spirituality legitimate taking revenge? For example, does my religion or spiritual practice endorse vengeance in war, against terrorism, or by capital punishment? Or does it unconditionally and universally take a stand against it—and help me live that commitment? Flavius Josephus, a Roman-Jewish historian of the first century, wrote in *Contra Apionem*: "I suppose it will become evident someday that the laws in the Torah are meant to lead to a universal love of humanity."

EGO

Any discussion of our will to retaliate leads straight to the door of the narcissistic ego, the pal of division and opponent of oneness. Vengeance is a tool of the entitled ego whose favorite pastime is payback. The turning of a heart from retribution to reconciliation means adopting a new standard in our relationships: loving back, not hurting back. It will take nothing less to accomplish this than the total demolition of the narcissistic ego, the gold-medal winner at getting even. We then let go of vengeance, in attitude and deed, and possibly even disarm it in others, rather than join its never-ending futile game.

Let's look at two of the options we will explore in this book: at a minimum, case-by-case nonretaliation, and maximally, a lifelong change:

- We refrain from retaliating this time. Each time we do that we reduce the influence of the vengeful ego on our decisions. Instead, we choose a nonviolent way of resolving a conflict. This will take *effort* and putting our choice into action.

- We can make an ongoing commitment unconditional and universal, adopting a new standard we will live by: reconciliation and forgiveness, which is what happens when we recover from the ego's addiction to revenge. Letting go of retaliation takes nothing less than a whole new orientation of ourselves in relation to others. This will be a spiritual advance, an awakening, a shift we do not make happen but nonetheless happens. Such a total transformation is a spiritual gift to us, a *grace*.

GRACE

Let's now define two terms we will be using in this book, *grace* and *loving-kindness*. *Grace* refers to the gift dimension of life, moments and happenings that help us, prompt us, and evince more than we thought was in us. Grace is free to us, so it is not produced or attained by effort. Grace is not an effect, not an award based on exertion, merit, or accomplishment. We have all had something happen to us that helped us and we know we did not cause it. We have accessed courage or wisdom we did not have before. We have felt involuntarily called, prompted, and activated. Those are examples of graces, the gift moments in life.

In accord with our own belief system, we may see grace simply as happenstance or synchronicity. We might also see grace as welling up from Mother Earth, or as a blessing from God, assistance from Buddha, or a gift from a higher power than the ego. Assisting forces, powers that kick in beyond our own effort, are anywhere we look for them, with any name we give them, or with no name at all. St. Teresa distinguished effort from grace in a charming way. She said that when she watered her garden, that was effort, and when it rained, that was grace. She knew she needed both if buds were to blossom.

When we are graced with a shift in our mindsets and behaviors in favor of nonviolent loving-kindness, we have awakened. This is an awakening as what happens in the morning: we don't make ourselves wake up, it simply happens. Then, like Alice in Wonderland, we find ourselves released from a world that never did make sense. We have made the luminous journey from vengeance to loving-kindness. In other words, we ourselves have become a grace to the world around us.

Ultimately grace is a mystery, but we can say it is:

Something,
we know not what,
is always and everywhere
lovingly at work,
we know not how,
to make us more than we are now,
to make the world more than it is yet.

LOVING-KINDNESS

In Buddhism, the loving-kindness practice, also called *metta*, consists of sending/intending love and happiness to ourselves and others. *Metta* is a Pali word meaning goodwill, friendliness, or loving-kindness. In this book I suggest a loving-kindness practice that looks like this: we send love and happiness first to ourselves, then to those close to us, then to those toward whom we are neutral, then to marginalized people—that is, those who are "othered," looked down on, or oppressed by society—then to those we don't like or who don't like us, even enemies and those who have been hostile, aggressive, or vengeful toward us, and finally to all beings. We can engage in the practice with daily aspirations of goodwill that we send to, feel for, and show to all those circles of people in our lives and in the world. We can do this each day and in challenging relationship moments throughout the day as well. The practice of loving-kindness makes us channels of grace. This is how grace and loving-kindness become one life-enriching experience. We also are aware in this practice that if we are sending love and happiness, we must already and always have them inside us. What a boost to our spiritual self-esteem!

But a loving-kindness practice does not end with aspirations. We live it out in daily life by showing love in spiritually evolved ways: unconditional, universal, and unending. We move from vengeance to forgiveness, from excluding to including, from hate or indifference to a caring committed connection, which is the very definition of unconditional love.

We have heard the phrase *unconditional love* so often in the self-help movement. Did we ever apply it to letting go of retaliation? In our Buddhist practice did we fully get that loving-kindness is the opposite of retribution? In our religion or spirituality did we see that divine love means no more hurting others? In intimate relationships did we ever realize that revenge is the opposite of love? We will explore these self-challenging questions in the pages that follow.

NOT A STRATEGY

A commitment to nonviolent loving-kindness in all our relationships makes no promise that we will find a sense of satisfaction or feel we have been justified when we are wronged. We may not even find safety. Perhaps just the opposite will occur, as was the experience of Buddha, Jesus, Gandhi, and Martin Luther King Jr. The practice of nonretaliation is not a strategy to acquire satisfaction for wrongs or even to survive, it is how we show love in a world of hurt and betrayal. A commitment to nonretaliation, to going beyond retaliation, is entirely a spiritual dedication born of an awakened conscience. It is not a tactic to be sure we will win, to get things to run as we want them to, to make things come out our way, or to show we are more advanced than other people. Likewise, we do not lose hope when our calling to nonviolence and nonretaliation does not seem to be making a difference in the world. Our commitment is not based on successful results but on having a heart of peace no matter its impact, no matter its failure to ripple.

I am often asked in workshops I present on the topic of letting go of retaliation: What if this unconditional love doesn't work to change the situation or the person who is offending you? There is no guarantee that nonretaliation will change the way others behave toward us. We love not on the condition that it will work in our favor or change someone. We don't allow others to keep hurting us, but we let go of hurting back. We do this only because we are now committed to loving without reserve. Our commitment to love is also part of not giving up on anyone. This is how love without conditions creates the condition of hope in humanity.

In mature spiritual consciousness we have no need for external validation of our calling to loving-kindness over revenge. This earth, with its evolutionary drive to survive and thrive, is our witness.

LOVE AND HURT

We have all heard the reminder to people who are being abused by family or partners: love is not supposed to hurt. Retaliation not only hurts but is meant to hurt. It includes harboring ill will and the choice to inflict pain on a transgressor. Retaliation is a dish, hot or cold, that has no place at the banquet of love. Our hooray for successful revenge is the death knell of love. We will keep coming back to one question in this book. Our biggest conundrum in loving is the question of why we are vengeful even in our intimate relationships. What puzzles me most is how we can say we love someone and yet keep engaging in love's antithesis, payback. Shakespeare noticed this contradiction too:

It is a quarrel most unnatural,
To be revenged on him that loveth you.[1]
—*Richard III*, act 1, scene 2

As long as we are retaliating, we are not loving. All we have is one hand slapping rather than two hands holding. We sometimes may retaliate against those we don't like, which seems to the ego to be quite justified. When we notice that we retaliate also against those we love, within a family or in any close relationship, we come face to face with a challenging question: Has lasting, trustworthy, sincere love truly taken hold in us?

Part of my writing process is to send to some wise friends and colleagues paragraphs in which I explore new ideas. I sent this introduction to my friend Brian, who wrote back:

I think there is something to look at in the term "falling in love." Falling admits to dropping to the bottom of something, the bottom where eventually we encounter things like anger, hostility, retribution, revenge, all those bottom dwellers. Too often we are tripped up by these conditions, as falling in love is passive, allowing entry to those ugly traits. Rising in love, however, is another possibility for us. It seems to me that there is a whole lot of fear involved in falling in or out of love. Whereas rising in or out of love, there is no fear, only enlightenment. Do I climb over my many small ego-selves (retaliation, retribution, revenge) to rise in the love into which I fell? Or, do I wander in this bottom place, alone in my retribution?

I found Brian's comments both touching and right on the mark. I see also, with a smile, that he too ends up asking rhetorical questions. I guess they are the only kind that are appropriate in a world of such mysteries as love and revenge.

LOVE NEEDS TENDING

Sooner or later in life we realize that love won't take care of itself. It is not like a weed that survives on its own with no help from a gardener. It is like an orchid that requires skilled and attentive care. Like flowers, children, and democracy, love requires conscious and continuous tending. Partners or friends who don't stay vigilant in cultivating their garden of ongoing, caring, and committed connection soon see it overgrown or gone altogether. When partners spend time caretaking a relationship, love matures, blooms, and thrives. It takes moving from payback to love back, every time.

What I am proposing here is that love itself is vulnerable. It needs constant care from us so that it won't deteriorate into hurt, jealousy, retribution, or worse, malice. Love is like a rose, beautiful in all its phases from budding to fading. But it will renew itself only if we remain alert and faithful to caring for it.

THAT SWEET FEELING

Biologically, revenge feels good. The plan for or success at achieving revenge stimulates neurons in the caudate nucleus, the part of the brain having to do with a sense of pleasure and reward. That is the same part of the brain that lights up when we are excited about an opportunity to feed any of our addictions—including the one to retaliate. However, the pleasurable reward experience in the brain is short-acting and we soon go back to our stressed baseline.

There are neurological elements in the entire retaliation experience. For instance, the right temporal parietal junction is involved when we cast blame or pass judgment on others' moral intentions and behavior. It is also true that letting go of retaliation and practicing unconditional forgiveness benefits our health, boosts our immune system, and reduces stress. Letting go of retaliation is likewise crucial to the success of the social contract that can only thrive on harmony and cooperation.

HITCH A RIDE

In this book I honor many traditions, especially Christian and Buddhist, two of the main sources of wisdom I have benefited from over the course of my life (not counting poetry). I am making no attempt to proselytize in this book. Both advocate letting go of retaliation in favor of forgiveness and loving-kindness. I see these practices as our best path to accessing the justice, peace, and love within every one of us and then heralding those same three joys to the world. Finally, it will take a conscious and honest safari into who each of us is and why we do what we do if we are to ever free ourselves from vengefulness or recognize its disastrous results in our souls and in the world around us. We will then ask ourselves if a life of love will, for us, be sweeter than revenge. We will even take a closer look at the expression "Revenge is sweet." Here is the quotation from Milton's *Paradise Lost*:

> Revenge, at first though sweet,
> Bitter ere long, back on itself recoils . . . [2]

What is it about us that would change the first line and omit the final line?

ONE

Understanding Retaliation

IN THIS CHAPTER we convene the Vengeance family who live in or around us. We will first meet the parents, Revenge and Retaliation. We will then encounter their children, Punitiveness, Hate, Evil, and Vengeful Ego. Let's visit without exonerating any of them but also with compassion for them. Our fearless clarity helps us with the former. Our spiritual practices help us with the latter.

We all know what retaliation is: you hurt me, so I hurt you. Retaliating is something like playing a game of dodgeball in which you hit me and then I hit you—but in that game there is no intent to harm. Retaliation is motivated by anger and includes the intent to harm. Aggression from you leads to aggression from me. Your aggression comes back at you from me. Retaliation thrives on *opposition*, the opposite of the oneness and harmony that makes for a trustworthy love. It is reciprocated aggression— aggression-provoked aggression with the intent to even a score, to show payback in kind. The aggressive behavior can be anything from criminal assault to snubbing.

In some instances there is no aggressive action on our part, but still there is what feels like retaliation coming at us. For instance, some people are mean or aggressive toward us just because they don't like us or because they envy us. Some people are dead set against us because of their bias toward us. They feel the need to react aggressively toward us just because, for instance, we are of a certain color, religious or political view, sexual orientation, gender, or for any other reason. We aroused a hostile, bigoted, or envious ego and it hit back at us for being us, not for anything we did. This aggression is not technically retaliation but certainly comes across that way. Likewise, controlling people might get back at us for not folding to their wishes or for defying or displeasing them.

Retaliation is the inflicting of harm or damage as a response to a *perceived* injustice. The judgment of what constitutes an offense or injustice is subjective. We, not a law, judge, or mediator, decide on the guiltiness or aggression in the other person. Retaliation thrives on inference and interpretation, which is another reason we may not be able to trust our subjective belief about the nature or reality of an injustice toward us. This is where dialogue is crucial in relationships. We can ask, "Did you mean to hurt me?"

Retaliation is an in-kind response to an offense or grievance. We react with a hurt for a hurt, a damage for a damage, an annoyance for an annoyance. Here we see the difference between ordinary aggression and retaliation: Aggression is hostile and injurious behavior, for any reason. Retaliation is aggression that is specifically triggered, provoked by an action that caused us pain. Retaliation as payback for an injury or injustice includes a deliberate choice to cause pain in the other person, the opposite of what a person committed to act with love would do.

Sometimes, as we saw above, the retaliatory response is equal to the offense: we do to others what they did to us. "He was late last time, so I will keep him waiting now." "She did not call me back soon after I called her, so I won't call her back soon either."

Payback can be more or less injurious than the original transgression: we are not as aggressive or more so than fits the bill. Throughout this book we also keep in mind that retaliation in general may follow both upon injuries against us as well as those against anyone who matters to us.

The word *retaliation* is from Latin: *re* means "back" and *tal* means "suchlike." We do such to others as they did to us—that is, aggression for aggression. We might also say it is a metaphor referring to arranging an equal tally. Society's laws and court sentences are meant to create proportionality regarding wrongs and the righting of wrongs. They act impartially and set limits on retaliation while nonetheless confirming its legitimacy.

The ancient phrase *lex talionis* refers to "the law of talion"—that is, payback in kind. That law was meant to ensure a sense of fairness: only take one eye for one eye, not two eyes for one—state-approved retribution. Capital punishment legitimates taking a life for a life. Nowadays, we would find it monstrous, however, for a court to cut out the eye of someone who took the eye of his victim. Yet many of us take in stride the taking of a life for a life.

Once we embrace the spiritual practice of going beyond retaliation, we no longer see capital punishment as legitimate. It shows itself for what it is: grossly primitive and vengeful cruelty, state sanctioned. Spiritual practices are meant to move us away from vengeful punishment. Then capital punishment is no longer a solution we support. We might even take a public stand against it in favor of alternatives like life in prison or, if possible, a corrective program. Shakespeare in *Henry V* refers to such an alternative approach to a criminal facing mortal punishment:

> You show great mercy, if you give him life,
> After the taste of much correction.[1]

OTHER ANGLES

Retaliation is not only a psychological experience, it is also a lop-sided way of *communicating*. Retaliation is meant to show those who offend us that we have been hurt. Our way of declaring this could of course be a straight-up telling others about how their aggression landed on us, rather than a striking back.

Retaliation is also meant to be a deterrent against further injury: "If you mess with me, you will pay big time!" In retaliation we believe that if we hurt the hurters, they won't hurt us again. It's certainly a primitive way to display our suffering or give a warning. We notice also that some aggressive behaviors upset the social contract, an agreement in a community about the duties of the citizenry so we can all be safe, free, and secure. Then retaliation might be seen as a deterrent that safeguards the contract.

Massive retaliation is disproportionate retaliation. This refers to a nation's commitment to over-the-top, extreme retaliation if another nation were to attack. If both nations espouse massive retaliation, then bilateral escalation results. Each nation is hoping for deterrence—that is, that the other will back off once it sees how seriously it takes its plan for payback. Now that we have nuclear weaponry, massive retaliation means the end of life on our planet.

Retaliatory behavior is often a compulsive, knee-jerk reaction: "I feel obligated to make it right. I have to retaliate; I don't feel it is a choice. I am hell-bent on getting back at the people who harmed me." This is equivalent to what Freud called "the repetition compulsion." Of course, the one we retaliate against may be driven by an identical compulsion to get back at us!

Another word for retaliation is "retribution." It is literally a paying back. Originally it meant the same as requital, returning good for good and evil for evil, but now it refers only to the latter.

Retribution is from the Latin *re + tribuere*, to allot or assign back to the person what she is owed. The goal of retribution in a court setting is to ensure that the punishment is objective, commensurate to the offense. In opposition to this, revenge is emotionally driven, subjective, and seeks to inflict pain and punishment without calculating what is proportionate or even legitimate.

Most people who retaliate do so when we:

Offend them in a major way
Bruise their ego
Harm them
Hurt their feelings
Fail them
Betray them
Reject them
Damage their reputation
Are disloyal
Make them lose face in front of others

Some people retaliate when we:

Offend in a minor way
Slight their ego
Best them in a competition
Give them a reason to envy us
Disagree with them, especially in front of others
Not take their part in an argument
Not stand up for them
Won't hate the people they hate
Confront, criticize, or even give them feedback
Cut them off in traffic
Rebuff their sexual or romantic interest in us

RETALIATION AND REVENGE

We have all heard the expression "with a vengeance," meaning to come down especially hard or cruelly on offenders. Vengeance is another word for revenge, but it hits with a heavier thud than the retaliation we have been describing.

In this book, we use the words *retaliation* and *revenge* interchangeably. Technically, however, revenge is described nowadays as a more severe form of retaliation:

- Retaliation can be satisfied once and for all; revenge is usually insatiable, can't get back at you enough.
- The goal of the retaliator is to have the punishment fit the crime. It is commensurate, an eye for an eye. But revenge disregards the math and is okay with increasing the rancor it ultimately fails to resolve. It is assassination for an eye. We may also recall here Gandhi's saying that "an eye for an eye makes the whole world blind."
- Retaliation can be brief and unplanned. Revenge is usually long-term and executed with careful planning, as reflected in the mean-spirited saying "Revenge is a dish best served cold."

The words *revenge*, *vindictiveness*, and *vengeance* are all from the same Latin word *vindicare*—"to lay claim to, vindicate, punish"—signifying a response that is considered justified because of a transgression or because our ego has been outraged or has lost face. An example is an "honor killing" within or between families in some parts of the world today.

We recall that the First Amendment to the US Constitution states our right "to petition the government for a redress of grievances." Since society has a court system and laws to handle injury cases, revenge for an injury is, in effect, taking the law into one's own hands. It is the act of a mutineer, a vigilante, or an insurrectionist.

When revenge for justice passes from one generation—or one person or group—to the next, it is called a feud. In a feud, people in the present demand redress for the harm done to their ancestors or fellow group members. An example is the famous Hatfield-McCoy feud. Feuding people believe they have a right, even an obligation, to take revenge on the descendants of those who affronted their family members, ancestors, or confreres years ago. Revenge has a long lifespan.

REQUITAL AND RETALIATION

We can distinguish retaliation from requital—that is, responding in kind to both positive or negative experiences, hurt or help, good deeds or ill. Requiting is an innate, hardwired capacity in all of us, equal to that of revenge. We are DNA-geared to reciprocity. We are inclined to hurt those who hurt us, a negative reciprocity. We are inclined to be kind to those who are kind to us, positive reciprocity. Returning a favor while feeling gratitude for it, another innate inclination, is an example of positive requiting.

Retaliation has one subheading: evil for evil. Requiting has two subheadings, evil for evil and good for good. We might say requital is the genus and retaliation is one species of it. In both, an action is matched with a like action. Our response is conditioned by others' actions: "If you hurt me, I hurt you. If you help me, I help you. If you scratch my back, I scratch yours." *Requital reminds us that if a retaliator were truly logical about the legitimacy of returning a frown for a frown, he would also return a smile for a smile—every time!*

Yet we also have the capacity to go a step beyond requital. We have the capacity not to repeat harm that was done to us. We can respond to others in accord with a personal standard: "No matter how you treat me, I treat you, and all people, with respect. If you are violent, I attempt to stop you, but nonviolently." Living by a standard shows personal integrity. What others do, how they behave, does not have to condition or dictate what we do. We can show up with our own creative alternative action. Along these lines, we recall that ancient Romans were notable for two standards, both indicative of requital: fierceness toward enemies in a battle and clemency toward them in their defeat—not kicking them when they were down.

BEST SERVED COLD

An avenger usually wants to see the target person suffer, especially in an unguarded moment. This may explain the heartless phrase "Revenge is a dish best served cold." The vengeful person wants not only to rejoice in the exacting of a reprisal but also to gloat over the surprised and pained look on the face of his enemy. Revenge is deeply intertwined with a false sense of power: "You made me look bad, weak. Now I will show you I am the dominant one. I get my power back by payback. I put you in your place— that is, below me." This is bully power for humiliation, not restorative power for reconciliation.

When an ego can inflict damage on the other equal to that inflicted on itself, it has equalized the playing field. We believe that when we retaliate we are no longer smarting victims but smart, re-empowered victors. Revenge is about restoring egoic power to the victim rather than creating mutual power for better relating in the future.

Sometimes revenge or retaliation does not require that the other knows it is happening. I recall an episode of the TV series *All in the Family* in which the bigoted main character, Archie Bunker, insults an Orthodox Jew. The slighted man replies in Yiddish. When Archie looks at him quizzically and asks: "What the hell does that mean?" The man replies: "You'll never know, but boy did I get even!"[2]

Seeing a transgressor "get his" may give us satisfaction even when we are not the ones who execute it. Seeing others being punished lights up the left ventral striatum, a reward circuit. This may also help explain why people in the past lined up so excitedly to see a hanging. The state is exacting revenge in our name against the one who harmed us or our society. Motives for watching executions vary of course. Families of the victims may believe they are finding closure. The implication is that making others suffer will dispel our own grief. What irony, since grief is the very process that will effectively grant closure.

On this topic of spectator events, let's look at boxing and prizefighting. Both engage the metaphor for retaliation: when hit, hit back. Boxing is a legitimate sport using protective gear to prevent serious harm to the body. Prizefighting is pommeling with intent to cause serious damage to the body. What part of the human soul would want to pay and bet while two guys beat each other to a pulp in a ring or a combat cage of brutality?

ONLY WE?

Are humans the only ones who practice revenge? Charles Darwin, in *The Descent of Man*, wrote: "It has, I think, now been shown that man and the higher animals, especially the Primates, have some few instincts in common. . . . They practice deceit and are revengeful; . . . they feel wonder and curiosity."[3] So we are not the only ones who retaliate. Primates, other animals, insects, and birds also seem to hold grudges and to engage in revenge. For example, crows recognize and remember those who harm them and will come after them aggressively. Elephants have a long-term memory for abuse and may attack their abusers. Wolves may show retaliatory behavior toward humans who harm them or their pups.

There are, however, major differences between the human and animal styles of revenge. Animals don't gleefully plot their revenge, they only act on instinctive impulse. They also do not seek the personal sense of reward and pleasure that humans feel in calculating a plan for recrimination and seeing it happen. Calculated revenge happens most often among humans who have time on their hands or are in a privileged position. Wild animals, and some people, have to put all their attention on survival, so the plan for revenge is not so elaborate. Animals do not act aggressively just for the sake of it; they do no more than what is expedient for the maintenance of survival. Likewise, unlike humans, animals retaliate once, not over and over. They do not intend any more harm than what legitimately fits with their goal of halting or preventing aggression. Human revenge can be mean, malicious, or cruel—these are all qualities of immoral behavior. Animal behavior does not include that element.

WE GET BETTER AT IT

The means of revenge have become more and more sophisticated over the centuries. At first, revenge could only happen in face-to-face encounters. Now powerful or wealthy individuals can hire someone to perpetrate their revenges. In addition, communication tools for revenge have advanced in number and quality. Poison pen letters were followed by gossip columns and telephone vitriol. Today we can use social media not only to retaliate against our offenders but also to shame them to a worldwide audience.

Likewise, we see a progression in the weaponry available for vengeance. Our earliest ancestors used hands and clubs. As revenge continued to escalate, so did the means of achieving it. We moved from clubs to arrows to guns to drones and nuclear armaments. These most recent weapons kill vast numbers of people, not only the specifically named "offenders." Commitment to revenge easily legitimates such collateral damage. Since we too can be collateral damage, murder and suicide, the ultimate results of revenge, perpetuate the gruesome tug of war in which no side wins. We keep in mind regarding the evolution of weaponry that society advanced in the opposite direction in its forms of punishment: we moved from beheading to life in prison or lethal injection.

THE DEHUMANIZED ZONE AND WAR

Politically, revenge thrives on dehumanizing others so that the voice of our humanist conscience can be disabled. For instance, we mispronounce the enemy's name and use derogatory epithets: Veet-nahm instead of Vietnam, Eye-rack instead of Iraq, Krauts instead of Germans, Gooks instead of Asians.

We get a free pass to do anything to dehumanized enemies, as, for instance, in war that legitimizes killing, pillage, rape, arson, torture, and other gruesome crimes. As avengers we are innocent of all wrong because the objects of our aggression are not worthy of a humane or merciful response. Dehumanizing is the most terrifying example of being caught in the illusion of separateness. It grants full permission to engage fiendishly in the most repulsive horrors of war.

Soldiers may be dehumanized as well when they are ordered to commit heinous acts. Soldiers coming into a war are, in effect, forced to retaliate when they themselves were not offended. They have to act like executioners, but without the taste—or reason—for it. The act of dehumanizing soldiers also applies to our own view of them. We dehumanize them when we take news reports of civilians being killed in stride. The implication is that it is wrong to kill civilians, but the killing of soldiers is legitimate and irrelevant. Our belief that soldiers, unlike civilians, sign on for and assume the risk of death only shows how we dehumanize them even as we keep seeing that war is not a humane solution to conflicts.

We saw another example of dehumanization thinking with respect to both soldiers and civilians after 9/11 when the United States went to war in Iraq on a false claim that it was avenging those killed by al-Qaida. We soon lamented that we had retaliated against the wrong country. When our commitment is to the practice of loving-kindness toward all beings, attacking *any* country is unacceptable.

We have recourse to judicial and diplomatic alternatives to war, including the United Nations and the International Crime Court in The Hague. Aggression and retaliation bypass those options and contribute to disempowering them. The fact that alternatives to war may not be trusted as effective strategies does not revoke the *moral* issue in this discussion. And, of course, we know that war cannot be trusted to work either.

Our survival calling as humans is roundtable dialogue among nations to explore the entire spectrum of possibilities regarding modes of defense. A binary solution is insufficient. Putting our many heads together to deal peaceably with conflicts is our only chance to save our planet. That may not be the goal of the human ego, though it is the goal in our Buddha nature.

Yuval Noah Harari, at the Tel Aviv peace rally "It's Time" in July 2024, wisely said: "War is not a law of nature, it is a human choice. Every moment we can choose differently and start making peace. All wars have led us to the abyss. It is time to give peace another chance."[4] Like all those who speak for peace, his voice cries in the wilderness. His message will sound Pollyannaish to a majority of people, hard to be believed. The frightening alternative, however, is to join the march toward death, which is the ineluctable objective of war and revenge. Here is where our compassion for that majority needs to open into peaceful protest and indefatigable conferencing for nonviolent solutions to international conflict. We may or may not convince, but we might influence. And no matter what, in spiritual consciousness we never give up on the possibility of the transformation of anyone and everyone.

MINORITIES TOO

What is true of so-called enemies in war also applies to minorities against whom we are prejudiced. We implicitly dehumanize them when we refer to them with scorn and derision and find them unworthy of access to the full Bill of Rights. We may then feel justified in being vengeful and aggressive toward them. Our xenophobia makes us see difference as an assault. Revenge thrives on such myopia.

Ethnic groups that were once at the bottom of the social totem pole and have attained a higher tier of society might treat the next generation with the same derision and contempt that they or their parents endured. It's as if making it in society means becoming elitist and even hateful toward those on the lower rungs of the ladder of success, the rungs that so many of our immigrant families found themselves on in past decades. Some groups never get to climb the ladder but remain lower-class citizens across generations no matter what their education or financial status. We enact laws and use city planning to keep them in their place. We infringe on their voting rights to exclude them from full citizenship status or full participation in society. All this is about dehumanizing others for being born with a certain color, sexual orientation, gender, economic status, or religion.

The list of lower-class citizens is actually quite lengthy. It begins with women. They are objects of bias, especially in society, politics, churches, and workplaces. President Jimmy Carter spoke up regarding religious prejudice against women when he left the Southern Baptist Convention in protest in 2000:

> Male religious leaders have had, and still have, an option to interpret holy teachings either to exalt or subjugate women. They have, for their own selfish ends, overwhelmingly chosen the latter. Their continuing choice provides the foundation or justification for much of the pervasive persecution and abuse of women throughout the world.[5]

He reminds us that prejudice by respected groups induces dehumanizing policies and even validates reprisals if women seek equality.

Likewise, people in LGBT groups or who identify as in any way diverse are also dehumanized, disrespected, and deprived of the full array of their human rights. Groups that are marginalized are ultimately objects of some form of recrimination, directly or indirectly, by the privileged mainstream. Revenge is a weapon of choice in the arsenal of oppression. In addition, we have no rights when the exercise of them makes us liable to some form of legal recrimination or scorn.

Here are three possible reasons why our fear makes us believe we have to dehumanize marginalized groups:

* In personal interactions, we may need enemies and low-status people so we can displace our own aggression onto them, making them our scapegoats. In a family example, we are angry at dad but displace the anger onto our little brother—who will learn to do that to the next sibling in what becomes a pecking order rather than an orderly file of mutually loving family members. Likewise, in war, ten citizens of a town may be killed as scapegoats to make up for the one officer who was killed by the resistance.

* Politically, encouraging division in the population gives demagogues the opportunity to manipulate people's primitive fears in order to get themselves elected as liberators.

* Our leaders may need us to have an enemy from whom they can protect us and on whom they can wage war for venal purposes: they can then provide the profits of war to large corporations. This connection between war and money is not new. Here is Aeschylus, a Greek playwright who died in 456 B.C.E., on war in his play *Agamemnon*: "Only a spear and sword, and ashes in an urn! / For Ares, lord of strife, / Who doth the swaying scales of battle hold, / War's money-changer, giving dust for gold, / Sends back, to hearts that held them dear, / Scant ash of warriors, wept with many a tear. . . . "[6]

We recall Abraham Lincoln's commitment to act after the Civil War "with malice toward none, with charity for all." We can restate his words as a moral challenge: we hate no one, we show love to everyone. That is the style of justice; revenge does not go there. Revenge is to justice as a poisoned apple is to a Georgia peach.

TWO

Finding Another Way

WHEN OTHERS OFFEND US it feels unfair to us. Yet a given of life is that life is often unfair. We may choose to retaliate as a way to oppose that given. As we mature spiritually, a given leads instead to a response of "Yes, now what?" This is our question when we are offended or in response to retaliation. The "now what?" can become a fourfold practice: we grieve, we say "Ouch!" to the offender, we ask to open a dialogue, and we send loving-kindness and goodwill. The practice does not have to stop with personal interactions. It can also apply to mediations, international issues, court litigations, and organizational conflicts.

In this alternative program to retaliation we don't let others walk all over us, but we also don't just walk right back over them. We find a way to walk together toward a solution that works for both of us. To fight back nonviolently when someone is aggressive toward us is not retaliation when we simply fend off further aggression—that is, when we defend, not attack. We protect our boundaries, not letting abuse or offense happen or continue. We are also not enabling the aggressor to keep causing harm. To stop the fighting is to stop aggression. It becomes retaliatory when we strike back with a mean edge and we intend harm. To fight on is to further hostilities and cause damage.

In this, and in all the practices in this book, we remain aware that those suffering from trauma may not be ready to engage the whole practice or may not feel safe attempting it alone. Timing figures in for all of us. We take our baby steps unabashedly, and sometimes only those, or none, for the time being. And we trust there will always be time.

We also keep in mind, regarding dialoguing, that if the offending person refuses to hear us or does not want a dialogue with us, we affirm that we will stand by and be ready for it in the future. If there is total silence or if we are shut down by the other, we let go without rancor and with goodwill. In Buddhist terms, we can also include that person in our own loving-kindness practice. Dialogue happens only with people we face and relate to. When the offender is a stranger, as in road rage incidents, dialogue is unnecessary, but loving-kindness is always a gift we can give.

PRACTICE

Going Beyond Retaliation

With all this in mind, let's look at the practice of going beyond retaliation. We engage in all four steps or however many of them are appropriate to the person or to the nature of the relationship:

1. We pause and let ourselves feel grief about our suffering, if only for a moment. Grief is a combination of sadness that we were injured, anger at the one who inflicted the injury, and fear that it might happen again. A grief response exists on a spectrum. It can be based on anything from having our feelings

hurt to trauma from a deep betrayal. Our practice is simply to feel whatever we feel, in accord with the lightness or heaviness of the hurt, rather than immediately jump to payback.

2. We speak up and say "Ouch!" or the equivalent to the other person in whatever nonviolent form works for us. Since our practice happens in the context of mindfulness, we do not blame and judge the other but simply report our pain and show our wound.

3. We ask the person who offended us to engage in a dialogue with us to work things out. We do this without blame or judgment of the other person. Our goal in a dialogue with someone we relate to in daily life is reconciliation. This happens when we let go of resentment, ill will, blame, and any need to retaliate. Letting go of those four obstacles to love is what is meant by forgiving without condoning, which is the goal of the practice.

4. We silently include the offending person in our loving-kindness practice that day or simply send goodwill, compassion, and wishes for their enlightenment. A loving-kindness aspiration for someone might be: "May good things happen for you. May you find Buddha's way."

Here is a summary of the fourfold practice. It will help to write this out and look at it from time to time.

- We feel our grief.
- We say "Ouch!"
- We offer dialogue.
- We send goodwill.

Taking these four steps is how payback turns to love back. This practice is also a truly spiritual pathway to a sense of closure. Revenge won't get us there.

Tools We Will Need to Do the Practice

To practice feeling our grief we need to be in touch with our feelings—that is, acknowledge them by name and allow them to take their full course. This experiencing of our feelings will include a "yes" to the given of life that sometimes others may offend or harm us—and our reaction is our own. This prepares us for the next step.

To practice communicating our pain we need assertiveness. This is the ability to share our feelings directly and clearly. In spiritual consciousness we do this mindfully—that is, without judging, blaming, controlling, demanding, or aggression. We simply state the impact of the other's behavior on us.

To practice offering dialogue we need a commitment to nonviolent communication. Some of the skills for that way of dialoguing are included in the next section.

To practice sending goodwill we need the practice of loving-kindness. We wish goodwill and enlightenment to the other person; we forgive and let go. In addition, since the loving-kindness practice reaches out to all beings, it represents human solidarity when facing aggression, especially in the form of retribution that is directed at us. Thus, when someone penalizes us and we are in no way guilty, our practice extends to all people in that same predicament throughout the world. We support standing up against injustice everywhere, not only on our own doorstep. Spiritual practice always includes "more than" just personal concern. It is universal in its magnanimity.

These four skills—allowing and sharing our feelings, assertiveness, nonviolent communication, and loving-kindness as spiritual practice—have been introduced to us in a variety of ways by the self-help movement over the past twenty-five years. Now we put them together as one practice with four steps to free us from retaliation. We can see that each step is a skillful means to the practice of love. We love ourselves and others when we follow the four steps. We love others fearlessly when we can show them how they hurt our hearts and look for ways to bring our hearts together. The choice of retaliation destroys love. Coming to forgiveness is how love revives and thrives.

The Nonviolent Dialogue

- We tell our experience of what happened, including any "Ouch!" on our part.
- We reveal its impact on us, how we felt hurt.
- We relate our feelings of sadness, anger, and fear.
- We ask the other person to talk about what led to what came across as a hurt to us.
- We ask how we might have been offensive.
- We open to the other's feelings.
- We ask for or make amends if appropriate.
- We say that we want to feel safe in the relationship from now on and we discuss together how that can happen.
- We make an agreement for the future to let go of retaliation in favor of skillful communication that reveals our pain and offers dialogue.
- We admit, if appropriate, that we too have had vengeful thoughts toward others and have retaliated at times. We tell of our own move toward alternative ways to handle offense or aggression.
- Our introspection, which can be isolating, is complemented by an interaction that can lead to a restoration of togetherness.

REGARDING THE "OUCH!"

In our practice, we may not be ready to say "Ouch!" immediately. We may need to attend to our wounds, explore what triggered our experience, and be attentive to any trauma element in it. We may need a break and some space from the other person. Only then might we be ready to communicate our feeling of pain safely. This applies to any practice that includes pain and grief, especially if there is a trauma element. A pause is a necessary phase of healing. It is a path to clarity, recollection, and fully free decision-making.

A mindful pause is how we allow the triggering event to sit in our minds. We respond without the interfering layers of personal interpretation, judgment, fear, planning, control, anger, or the need to retaliate. This spiritual moment is the preamble to the assertive and psychologically healthy follow-up practices listed above.

Each of us has to ask, "What is my way of feeling grief? How do I feel the pain? It can be anything from using the word *ouch* to looking pained or shedding tears. What matters is that we are fearlessly reporting the impact of someone's aggressive action. Our "Ouch!" may not always meet with a cooperative or welcoming response from others. Some people don't want to see or hear about our feelings, much less explore them with us. They might also be insulted that we dared accuse them of wrongdoing at all. Instead of empathy from them we might even be met with its opposite, retaliation. It is up to us to know the other person's level of openness to dialogue and gauge our response accordingly.

Sometimes the most prudent course is not to say "Ouch!" Loving-kindness sometimes shows itself best by maintaining respectful silence. In any case, when letting go of retaliation is a standard we live by, we no longer need apologies from others to feel closure. Our practice gives us closure.

Codependent people may not feel comfortable with saying "Ouch!" Codependency includes having traits like these: We go out of our way to be nice to someone. We appease those who offend us rather than tell them of our pain. We let others take advantage of us. We continuously feel guilty that we have not given enough. We believe we always owe others but they never owe us anything. We keep giving more when we receive only less.

Codependent people will look for ways to appease others. Usually they will not dare to retaliate openly, as there is too much at stake, too much to lose. This is not the spiritual practice of letting go of retaliation. It does not come from an awakened consciousness, but from fear of abandonment. The work for codependent people is to grow in self-esteem and let go of the fear that holds them hostage.

GRACIOUS FORBEARANCE

An alternative or combinable practice to the fourfold practice is forbearance. It is defined in the dictionary as restraining oneself from a normal or customary aggressive reaction—for example, retribution when one is provoked to anger about unfairness or offensive treatment. In either case, we are magnanimously forgoing what we are owed or patiently tolerating an infraction. Forbearance does not mean putting up with aggression or letting others get away with injustice but only being compassionate and lenient in how we handle it.

The *Samdinirmocana Sutra* defines patience as forbearance when insulted. In matters of little consequence or toward people who mean no harm, forbearance and patience can be used as an alternative to the fourfold practice of grief, revealing one's pain, dialogue, and goodwill. We let go and move on with no resentment or plan for a later payback. Our experience can still include grief, but we keep it to ourselves or share it with a confidant.

As a second option, forbearance can be a step following the other four practices. Including it in our fourfold practice may give us a sense of closure, of inner peace, and of generosity.

Since forbearance is part of loving-kindness, we can call this practice, either alone or part of the longer practice, "gracious forbearance." The gracious forbearance practice combines kindliness, generosity, compassion, and patience, all features of our loving-kindness practice.

PRACTICE

Cultivating a Heart of Magnanimity

1. *Ask for Help from Assisting Forces.* We turn to a power higher than ego for the grace to activate our magnanimity and support us in showing it. We might also ask for pointers from friends who show magnanimity.

2. *Use Affirmations.* We affirm daily that we have the very qualities that describe magnanimity:

   - I am abundantly generous in spirit.
   - I am free from holding resentments, grudges, or envy.
   - I accommodate others' failings.
   - I am easily forgiving.
   - I accept the givens of life with equanimity.

3. *Act As If.* We simply act as if we are already magnanimous, and soon magnanimity will become second nature. Our behavior awakens our potential for magnanimity.

Thirteenth-century Zen master Eihei Dogen's "Regulations for the Study Hall" recommends magnanimity. We also notice that he includes the "act as if" behavioral change style:

> With mutual affection take care of each other sympathetically, and if you harbor some idea that it is very difficult to encounter each other like this, nevertheless display an expression of harmony and accommodation.[1]

The threefold practice—ask, affirm, act—applies to any virtue we seek to install into our daily life. We all have every virtue as potential. Practices activate them from dormancy to display. No virtue is beyond our reach—a basis of unreserved hope for a humanity capable of justice, peace, and love.

RETALIATION AND EGO

We have seen how the inflated—that is, narcissistic—ego plays a central role in retaliation. Let's look now at what we mean by the mindset called "inflated ego" and how it more specifically coincides with the choice to retaliate.

A healthy ego can be described as a feature of the executive function of our brain. This is the part of us that thinks rationally, assesses accurately, acts responsibly, fulfills our life goals, speaks assertively, builds effective relationships, protects the rights of ourselves and others, and has healthy self-esteem. Its favorite sport is creating harmony.

Retaliation is the favorite sport of the narcissistic ego. That ego is a mindset we cultivate and empower over the years. Egotists are not fun—or safe—to be around because they

- think only of themselves
- do whatever promotes their own sense of superiority, benefit, or advancement
- feel compelled to be in control
- feel justified in acting aggressively or dishonestly to get their own way
- feel entitled to be honored by others without having to honor them in return
- can't stand being bested or crossed in any way

- can't receive feedback or critiquing
- engage in projection without foundation: "You are the one with the big ego!"
- can't say "I'm sorry" and don't see any need to, no matter how they may have hurt others
- permanently hold it against someone who has offended them
- refuse to make amends to anyone
- believe that others owe them but they owe no one
- can't be called on any of the above

This list also describes the mindset of retaliation. It is precisely the sense of entitlement that convinces such an ego that it has the right and obligation to exact revenge. The arrogant ego loves to feel triumphant over anyone who dares to cross or wrong it. Being able to feel the reward of retaliation gives such an ego its sense of power—which is ultimately illusory because it is the street-bully version of power. The saying "Power corrupts" refers also to revenge that corrupts our hearts: revenge corrupts; endless revenge corrupts endlessly.

To the narcissistic ego, losing face feels like losing control, being weak, and an insult to its entitlement. To save face—that is, to save ego by retaliating—restores the ego's sense of being back in control. Retaliating, however, proves to be an unskillful form of controlling. "Unskillful" is more than unsuitable; it is also ineffective—and the ego can't stand being powerless. The skillful practice is to disarm the ego and invest its powers into forming a healthy ego, one that acts cooperatively and generously. That is the mindset of self-giving rather than self-serving.

Our doctor performs a procedure that hurts. Yet we do not retaliate but take it in stride. So we know we can experience pain from someone without having to retaliate. But when the pain is also an affront to our ego, then we hit back.

Some ego-driven people perform acts of revenge with deadly

force. Duels, blood feuds, gang paybacks, honor killings, and war are violent rituals played out over the centuries and still happen today. They are ego-restoring in the euphemism of defending honor—that is, saving the inflated ego from the deflating it actually needs. We also notice in these violent rituals that for some people, the assertion and defense of ego is more important than their very lives.

A big ego certainly has no place in healthy relationships; it prohibits intimacy altogether. But there is a place for a swaggering ego. Rory McIlroy, the Irish golf pro, put it this way in comments he made at a tournament: "You know, I need that cockiness, the self-belief, arrogance, swagger, whatever you want to call it. I need that on the course to bring the best out of myself. So, you know, once I leave the golf course, that all gets left there."

Can the "I" of a fear-based ego loosen up so that a love-based I can emerge?

PRACTICE

Going Beyond Ego

Letting go of the will to retaliate takes the very same practices as letting go of egotism. Here are some I have used myself and shared over the years. These practices can simultaneously help us defoliate ego and dismantle the will to retaliate. At the same time, they help us build a healthy ego, one with self-esteem, humility, and loving-kindness. A sturdy commitment to these ethical choices also gives us the courage to face the worldwide revenge we so often see around us in these trying days.

1. Follow the Golden Rule: act toward others as you would want them to act toward you.
2. Keep the needs of others in mind, especially in little ways—this is an antidote to self-centeredness.

3. Find ways to maintain healthy self-esteem without showing off. It's okay to be a big shot, just don't act that way.

4. Let go of ranking, especially of elitism—that is, seeing yourself as above others for any reason, including because you follow a spiritual path.

5. Acknowledge not knowing something and show that you need support or help.

6. Take feedback as useful information, not as criticism, even when it is meant that way.

7. Apologize when you know you have harmed, offended, or retaliated against anyone. Open a dialogue that works toward repair of the relationship, including making amends as needed.

8. Let go of attempts to control, dominate, or manipulate others.

9. Give people leeway and make allowances for their errors rather than pointing out, or calling them out on, every little thing they do that irks you.

10. Welcome disagreement because it can lead to dialogue. In a discussion this puts the emphasis on arriving at common ground or learning a new truth rather than maintaining opposition or insisting on proving yourself right.

11. Cooperate rather than compete; collaborate rather than have to show that you know best.

12. In a group, give up having to take center stage. Trade in your own ego investment for the good of all concerned or for the accomplishment of the group goal.

13. Reconcile yourself to the givens that you will not always get your way, always win, always be liked, always be acknowledged, gain acclaim, or be appreciated.

14. Don't hold a grudge against those who wrong you, even when they won't admit it, and give up telling the story of how they offended you. Look for ways to reconcile rather than retaliate.

15. Remain on high alert for the entry of your reactive ego: the moment when you take what happened personally, become indignant, or interpret an action by someone as a slight to your dignity. Know your trigger points and limit your reactions.

16. When someone's ego is aroused toward you, do not dig your heels in or go nose to nose. Simply pause with compassion toward the pain in that person's ego reaction and treat it with loving-kindness, while nonetheless not putting up with any abuse.

17. In an intimate relationship, give up vindicating yourself in order to gratify your ego and instead let go of your ego to gratify the relationship. Become the protector of the partnership rather than the defender of your own ego supremacy.

18. Do good to those who hate you and pray or wish enlightenment for those who have betrayed, failed, or mistreated you.

19. See losing face (and all these suggestions) as welcome opportunities for growth in humility, a virtue that makes you more lovable. This is a bonus, of course, not a motivation for humility.

20. Discard the Ace (Arrogance-Control-Entitlement) of Ego for the Ace of Hearts.[2]

THREE

Feelings, Triggers,
and Traumas

ANGER IS DEFINED AS displeasure at a perceived injustice, like
when we believe we have been treated unfairly or cheated or betrayed. Feeling and expressing anger is how a healthy ego responds
to injustice. Anger is not synonymous with aggression. When our
anger includes hate or a will to retaliate it becomes abuse. This is a
style of the indignant ego that feels itself entitled to revenge at any
cost. Here is a chart I have updated over the years that may help
us see the difference between healthy anger and the retaliatory aggression that is abuse:

HEALTHY ANGER	AGGRESSION OR ABUSE (THE SHADOW SIDE OF ANGER)
Expresses a feeling in an authentic way	Becomes a tantrum in a theatrical way
Communicates, reports an impact	Puts down, bullies, or dumps on the other

HEALTHY ANGER	AGGRESSION OR ABUSE (THE SHADOW SIDE OF ANGER)
Asks for a change	Demands change or else threatens retribution
Respects the other's boundaries	Attempts to coerce the other
Is an I-Thou relationship: subject to subject	Feels like an I-It relationship: subject to object
Takes responsibility for the feeling	Blames the other person
Is based on an intelligent assessment	Is based on judgment, making the other wrong
Sees the other as a catalyst for our feeling	Sees the other as the cause of our reaction
Is about an action or word that felt unfair	Is about indignation, a bruised ego
Focuses on the here and now	Is contaminated by similar past events
Is brief and is let go of with a sense of closure (like a flare)	Is held on to as lingering resentment, obsession, or grudge (like a smoldering fire)
May be expressed with a red face, excited gestures, and a raised voice	May be expressed with a red face, menacing gestures, and a screaming voice
Says "Ouch!" assertively and respectfully while seeking a dialogue and sending goodwill	Is aggressive and adversarial, an attack based on ill will and perhaps with an intent to harm

Informs the other	Intimidates and threatens the other
Is nonviolent, in control, and always shown within safe limits (manages temper)	Is out of control, hostile, punitive, and may be violent (loses temper)
Maintains goodwill at all times	Maintains a mean or hateful ill will toward the other
Asks for accountability and amends to clear things up so forgiveness can happen	Seeks revenge, keeps holding something against the other, refusing to forgive or repair the relationship even when the other apologizes
Seeks mutual transformation	Wants to justify ourselves as in the right
Shows respect for the other as a peer	Shows contempt toward the other as a target
Aims at a deeper and more effective bond: an angry person moves toward the other	Wants to vent the rage no matter who gets hurt: an abuser moves against the other
Acknowledges the element of grief	Feels grief but masks or denies it
Coexists with love, maintains connection	Cancels connection
Is fearless	Is fear-based
Is a form of addressing, processing, and resolving an issue with spiritual consciousness	Is a form of avoiding one's own grief and distress about an issue with a refusal to work things out and thereby to grow spiritually

Courts and therapists sometimes direct out-of-control, violent people to classes that teach "anger management." In reality, anger does not need to be managed. That skill is already included in healthy anger. From my point of view, such programs are really about awareness of abuse and management of unhealthy ego reactions. Perhaps sometimes we could offer an adjunct or combined program and call it "Letting Go of Abuse and Retaliation."

The plan to retaliate is meant to save our ego from feeling *impotent* rage. We can escape any sense of vulnerability by immediately resorting to revenge. To the ego, that seems to clear the deck of its disturbing feelings. We even the score by circumventing uncomfortable feelings with swift payback. We feel safe again according to the inflated ego's definition of safety: being back in the driver's seat no matter who gets run over.

CONFRONTING THE BULLY

Ego-driven people might hold us hostage by threatening retaliation if we dare oppose, defy, or stand up to them. Here is an example. Within a relationship or family, or in any setting, there is sometimes a person who intimidates the other members of the group. Group members find themselves walking on eggshells. Often the intimidator threatens recrimination if the group does not adhere to his rules.

Such a bully has no real power over us. Any power he has is power that we give him. Until we find our assertive voice, the group or relationship dysfunction continues. It is our understandable timidity that keeps us from speaking up and from refusing to bow to his wishes. But wait! Is this entirely our own fear? Not at all. We are actually feeling his fear projected onto us. Just as the hurt hurt, the scared scare. A spiritual path to finding our own courage begins with feeling compassion for his and our suffering. This is how the practice of compassion can make us strong enough to take care of ourselves.

Let's also notice that when we let ourselves be bullied, more is happening than fear-based subjugation. We are *enabling* the bully to go on mistreating us and others. Likewise, when we allow others to use us as doormats, intimidate us, shame us, or in any way trespass on our rights, we are not simply becoming their victims. We are enabling our oppressors to be unfair and aggressive, not only to us but to any others they wish to harry. In other words, we are legitimizing, even sponsoring, the increase of violence in the world.

As children we may have based our moral decisions on rewards and punishments. As adults with mature spiritual consciousness we base our moral decisions on our cherished values and the principles that flow from them. This transition from the reward-punishment model to an awakened, conscience model is requisite if we are to embrace alternatives to retaliation.

WHEN WE RESENT

Ill will toward potential offenders or "enemies" can fester in us, and so we wait in the duck blind of resentment until our prey/enemy trespasses against us, then fire with the shotgun of revenge. We notice that nations also do this. They wait for an offensive action by their hated enemy and use it to justify pulling out the "big guns," striking back in full force, often with the help of allies who join in with equal vengefulness.

Resentment is like a treadmill of anger, a seething grudge that damages others. But our rancor also harms us. For example, in Twelve Step programs it is understood that holding on to our resentments puts us in danger of a relapse back into our addiction. In fact, on page 67 of the book *Alcoholics Anonymous*, we see that recovery includes letting go of retaliation altogether: "We avoid retaliation . . . putting out of our minds the wrongs others have done."[1]

In relationships, resentment eats away at any chance of intimacy or full-on commitment. It can thus be negatively "protective," ensuring that the closeness and commitment that we fear can't happen. Is that what we are up to when we hold on to resentments in our relationships?

Resentments are often unconscious or unrecognized. We then don't realize how much they steer our course toward vengefulness. For instance, we find ourselves glad to hear that something bad happened to a person we resent. That is an example of schadenfreude, glee at the downfall, misfortune, or suffering of others. It is retaliatory in its delight that "they got theirs." As we mature psychologically and spiritually, we fully attend to our long-held resentments—and look for ways to be released from their grip.

Deep-seated resentment, a grudge, includes egoic indignation based on our perception of an insult, injury, or a wrong against us. A full non-harming expression of anger can serve to quench our smoldering resentment. We know we have let go of resentment when a grievance becomes simply information rather than a portal into retaliation. As long as we remain triggered, we are still in the clasp of a vengeful ego.

A grudge is fundamentally an unending grievance. It is a silent form of retaliatory distancing. It affirms how justified we are in our resentment and how just it is to punish our offender for as long as possible. In mature spiritual consciousness, that weed wilts early. We notice then that the joy of letting go of a grudge is more fulfilling than the glee that comes with one more successful act of retaliation.

A clue that we may be holding a grudge is feeling the need to keep punishing the person who offended us. We might see this style in the mean behavior of an ex-husband who is still finding ways, sometimes through the children, to spite his former spouse. "Mean" is defined as petty, selfish, malicious, and hostile. Being mean is totally contradictory to loving.

In the 2006 film *The Painted Veil*, a husband uses the silent treatment to spite his wife for her affair, now ended. In one scene she directly asks him: "When are you going to stop punishing me?" Watching the film, I admired her assertiveness. The husband looked unhappy in every scene, and that reminded me that resentment is self-harming and ultimately a retaliation against oneself.

TRIGGERS

Triggers are events or traumas that lead to a strong reaction, especially that of sadness, anger, or fear—the three components of grief. Each of us has a set of personal triggers that may also activate our retaliatory impulse. We might then overdo it in how we retaliate. For instance, if one of our personal peeves is being rejected or abandoned, we are more likely to retaliate in an extreme way when either of those events happen. That can give us the go-ahead for vindictive anger. As we learn to widen our spectrum of tolerance for abandonment and rejection, we automatically let go of the need to retaliate.

For any of us, ordinary stresses and frustrations at home and work can be triggering. We can't avoid stress, but we can learn how to let it in without doing us in. One way this might happen is to have the exterior stress meet up with our inner resources, our skill set for handling anxiety-provoking situations. The practices in this book offer the skills to manage triggers, giving us a crucial advantage in letting go of resenting and retaliating.

Triggers are sometimes connected to our negative shadow side, unsavory traits we don't notice in ourselves but see quite vividly in others. These traits include ego entitlement to revenge and behaviors that are mean-spirited, abusive, unjust, unloving, or that violate human rights. When we are triggered into anger our shadow-side aggression may show up. Here is an example: Let's say that one of our trigger points is being taken advantage of. When that happens to us, we hit the ceiling with indignation and rage, and we immediately decide to retaliate. Actually, manipulating or fooling others, which are features of taking advantage of others, is a trait in us too. We don't see it, though, because it is unconscious, we haven't called ourselves out on it. When we are triggered by others' cheating us we tend to overreact because we are being forced to glimpse one of our own resident but hidden negative characteristics. Many acts of retaliation are in this category. We are getting back at others for something that is in us too but is yet unnoticed or denied or disavowed. We don't like being shown a mirror image of our own unappealing disowned self. And retaliation is the only way we have found to make the truth about us go away. As we keep seeing, there is a direct connection between having only retaliation as a choice and a woeful lack of imagination!

PRACTICE

When We Are Triggered

1. We allow ourselves to feel the anger, fear, sense of being attacked, or any other state of feeling. We show our emotion but in a way that is a communication rather than a form of aggression or retaliation. We remind ourselves that our feeling is our own rather than blaming the other person for it.
2. We assertively speak up about the impact of the other's behavior on us: "Here's how it feels at this end."
3. We ask for a time-out from our mutually aroused state until an effective dialogue can happen—when both of us calm down.
4. We look within to see if our reaction to the trigger was based on traumas from our own past, a bruised ego, or our own shadow side showing up in what we see in the other person. This will lead us to our personal work, preferably in the context of therapy.

TRAUMA AND REVENGE

We see that anger, resentment, grudges, and fear gather around trauma. Our trauma then sometimes leads to a desire for revenge against the perpetrator of the abuse.

Trauma requires grieving to be handled successfully. When all we aim for is avoiding our grief, the trauma remains frozen in us and is more likely to lead to post-traumatic stress and flashbacks. We are then triggered by new offending events that remind us of the original one. We might in such moments fail to ask ourselves the most healing question: "How can I let my trauma become transformative?" Allowing the full experience of our grief helps that happen. When we let ourselves feel what we have been hiding, the wallop of the trauma diminishes. We are no longer incapacitated by our wound.

Trauma thrives on denial, which is a way of perpetuating it. Trauma heals by authenticity, which is a path to transforming it. Unfortunately, trauma may prevent access to our inner resources and our higher or fully conscious mental functioning. When an offense happening in the present feels like a replay of our original trauma, we might be triggered into freezing—that is, into immobilization or a shutting down of our thinking brain. Later, when our thinking brain is back online, we regretfully think: "I should have said or done this!" In reality that would have been impossible because we did not have full access to rational thought.

If we have experienced trauma in the past, we may hold it against ourselves that we did not hit back then. But in most instances, immobilization or flight were safer protective strategies that prevented an escalation of abuse. Our bodies chose immobilization automatically as an *adaptive* measure, and so we are not victims. We were wisely choosing survival over dangerous retaliatory reactions. Now it is up to us to continue in that mode as a spiritual practice while still speaking our truth when we are ready to do so rather than freezing in fear.

People who feel consistently safe have been shown to speak up more easily, to handle trauma more effectively, and even to be less impacted or disabled by it. A sense of safety is necessary for human connection and for secure attachment.

Trauma distorts our sense of what new woundings from others are about by confusing present wounding with past ones. We lose our sense of the true impact of an event when it comes clothed in its former fashion. We also lose our sense of appropriate limits on how to respond in healthy ways. This helps us understand how unhealed trauma leads to overdoing our retaliatory responses to new afflictions, whether similar to the original or not. We also see how trauma and retaliation coincide and then collide.

Forgiveness may certainly be a tall order when we have suffered traumatic abuse. The familiar revenge thought pattern naturally comes to mind as a way to sidestep confronting our trauma: "I won't feel so bad if I can get back at the one who hurt me. I won't feel so bad if I can get back what they took from me. I won't feel so bad if I see them get theirs." Retaliation, however, is not a release from trauma inflicted on us by others. Nor does retaliation guarantee a sense of closure. But we can keep looking for new and healthy ways to close the books. Our work, best done in therapy, is long and complex. Yet seriously engaging in it can help us change our way of relating to our trauma and its perpetrators.

Traumas are not like wounds that fully heal but more like scars that last. I recall the last line of a poem by Emily Dickinson about working through grief: "It's better—almost Peace—."[2] Regarding the resolution of trauma, "better than before" and "almost resolved" may be as far as we can get and good enough. At other times it may not be enough. Only we know the full-length anatomy of our hurts, but even we can only guess at their consequences in the present. In our world of complexities, any of our experiences can only be described in approximations. In the world of healing trauma, the benefits only match the maladies in a hit-or-miss manner. This is not bad news, only a proclamation of the ever-elusive, ever-deepening mystery of human stories.

Some trauma is collective. For example, a nation that has been oppressed or has been victimized by genocide or by an unfair treaty after a war experiences trauma that passes from one generation to the next. Unfortunately, such nations may use war and vengeance to handle their collective trauma. That has not worked, as the history of Hitler's Germany has demonstrated. We notice that dictators manipulate collective trauma, often to the devastation of the populace and its democratic structures.

The work of Nelson Mandela and Bishop Tutu shows us how collective nonviolence can end divisions such as apartheid. Their Truth and Reconciliation Commission applied restorative justice by allowing perpetrators of the terrible crimes and abuses in South Africa to apply for amnesty based on confession and repentance. Implicit in the nonviolent project is recognizing that full reconciliation is a two-way street. It takes repentance by the perpetrator and forgiveness from the victim. When both parties engage in these spiritual practices, harmony can happen.

FOUR

When Retaliating
Becomes the Norm

NEWSCASTERS THESE DAYS so calmly report on reactive violence: "The US retaliated today against . . . " We take retaliation for granted in our society and in the world. The philosopher and journalist Hannah Arendt remarked that evil had become normalized, even acceptable, in World War II and after. Arendt called this "the banality of evil." That phrase certainly applies to the *normalcy of revenge* in our relationships and in international politics. Vengeance is taken for granted as right, justified, and hence acceptable in society, and most of us have consented to that view of it. We see revenge as the accepted norm—that is, what mostly happens and even should happen.

Arendt noticed that the word *evil* was not applied to events that were evil indeed. In the same manner, we don't call revenge by its rightful name. We use words like "justice," "deserved consequence," "legitimate reaction," "restoration of rights," or "righteous retribution."

Nowadays, we witness retaliation daily on TV or read about it in the newspapers. Revenge is endemic in our society and in most others. Revenge is the motivating factor in one of five murders in developed countries, and one of three in school shootings. Twenty percent of homicides in the United States are motivated by the desire for revenge. Likewise, physically aggressive sports include retaliatory attacks in almost every game. Will humans ever evolve so that revenge is no longer entertaining?

AT THE MOVIES

A simple example of the normalcy of revenge is visible in the storyline of so many movies. When we watch a crime drama, we expect that the bad guy will "get his" before the film ends. We may notice that we are glad to see that happen. We may even feel our own hands clenching as the payback occurs on screen, as if we were joining into it. We don't even think of the possibility of the criminal's redemption. What part of us is rejoicing in his getting only payback? When we see a character who is especially cruel in a film, we assuredly expect that he will be punished in a particularly gruesome way. Our insistence that the "punishment fit the crime" becomes an excuse for cruelty.

Yet we notice an exception: some villains, no matter their crimes, are so fascinating, and entertaining, that they escape for the sake of the sequel. The Joker in Batman films may be an example.

In most films we also notice a major difference between the retaliation styles of the hero and the villain. The hero retaliates against offenders, but only to right a wrong, not to be mean or cruel. Nor is he in any way excessive in meting out punishment. The hero has justice foremost in mind. The vengeful villain, on the other hand, is brutal in action and malicious in intent.

The filmmakers know our human penchant for revenge, so they make sure their story will satisfy our craving for it. None of this means we are evil people. But it does seem that we have inherited the feeling of revenge-as-justice from our cave-dwelling ancestors, and we are still holding on to it. We may also believe that revenge grants us catharsis, though it is simply the wish for revenge that is granted. We have erroneously equated retaliation with a contented sense of closure. Vengeance does not produce catharsis.

The silent film *Ashes of Vengeance* was made in 1923. *Rise of the Foot Soldier: Vengeance* was made in 2023. In the century between, there were hundreds of films in the same category. Revenge dramas, as far back as the ancient Greek plays and *Hamlet*, are still the most popular draws when it comes to entertainment.

Another sign of our partiality to retaliation is our fascination with fairy tales and Greek myths, which are replete with vengeance and punishment. Nemesis, the goddess of revenge, points out the enduring belief that divine approbation, even intervention, assures us in our vengeful purposes. (Ironically, it was Nemesis who punished the hubris-driven ego of Narcissus.) The ancients knew about and shared our predilection for satisfaction through revenge. Fairy tales, in particular, promise that revenge by magical powers guarantees that good people ultimately triumph over the injustices perpetrated on them by evildoers. Yet, adults have noticed that belief does not hold up in daily reality.

Myths and primitive stories are early forms of psychology. The vengeance-drenched tales are not about the actions of gods; rather, they describe us, our darkest fears and grimmest wishes. We fear being taken advantage of by others; we wish them pain in return and take pains to inflict it.

EXPECTED PAYBACK

Normalcy refers to the perennial status quo, the normal daily routine, what is expected to happen, and what we take for granted as a given in the vengeful world we share with others. Thus we will not be surprised when payback follows interactions like these with service people or authority figures:

- If we call customer service and we sound in the least critical or indignant, or if we raise our voice, we know we may likely be disconnected or be placed on hold for an inordinate amount of time. We have learned to be very meek when we call for help. The service person might also tell his fellow workers about us so they too can pay us back for daring to criticize their colleague.
- If we complain to the authority at our mother's nursing home about inadequate service, we may imagine someone on the staff will take it out on her when we are not around.
- When registering any complaint, giving feedback, or leaving a sincere note in the suggestion box, we believe we have to remain anonymous for fear of retaliation.
- We know we won't find work in our field if we dare to sue the agency we are employed by, even though such retaliation is illegal.
- When it is customary to slip money into the hand of someone from whom we want a special service, we know there will be a penalty if we don't. As another example, if we don't give the super of our building a monetary Christmas gift, we know we might receive less or slower service from him during the new year. Alternatively, we know we will receive better service for an especially hefty gift.

Or interactions like these in relationships:

- When someone ghosts us or is unresponsive around us we may automatically ask, "Did I do something to offend you?" We ask this because we know an offense on our part will most likely generate that kind of retaliatory response from the other person.
- If we keep winning in a competition with someone, we know there might be retribution coming our way.

- If we trigger someone with a big ego or paint a person into a corner—that is, make them lose in a way that feels humiliating—we expect payback to come at us sooner or later.
- When someone dislikes or envies us we expect that aggression may come our way.
- People may use social media to do us in if we offend them.

Or interactions like these close to home or worldwide:

- In some sports events it is taken for granted that players are violently retaliatory toward one another.
- When it is impossible to retaliate against the wrongdoer, the offended person may take revenge against non-offending others, which is a form of displacement. The injured ego may decide: "I want to hit someone, anyone!" (It is fascinating that macaques and other primates will retaliate against a weaker or lower-status member of the tribe if they can't cause harm to an offender directly.)
- Psychology proposes that men who were sexually abused in childhood by males might be strongly biased against or even seek to harm gay men. (We keep in mind here that it has not been proven that abuse in childhood necessarily leads to abusing others.)
- When we hear of a murder, we presume that the victim must have done something to trigger someone's revenge.
- The adage "You will kill more flies with honey than with vinegar" shows that we know that any aggression on our part will lead to retaliation. It may also show that we understand our need to placate in order to avoid possible retaliation.
- "You can be sure that if you don't give me what I want, I will not give you what you need." This vengeful threat is especially dangerous when it comes from an authority figure.

- Voters know that a presidential candidate who is antiwar or antiretaliation has no chance of winning.
- We believe that anyone who speaks up against a mob-favored authority figure will receive hate letters and death threats.
- We take it for granted that if a candidate says he will retaliate when he takes office, he will.
- A leader who invades a sovereign nation threatens to use nuclear arms if other nations support the invaded country. (Here we see how revenge can happen in the style of extortion so that the world is held hostage by a threat.)
- In international disputes we understand that revenge is common and presume that it is considered legitimate.
- We believe, or our leaders believe, that nationalism and the outdated notion of a "just war" justify entry into a war.
- We take for granted that there are and will be wars over religion.
- We believe that "God is on our side," which gives our nation a hall pass from divine authority to take revenge. We don't allow ourselves to see that a God who takes sides is not a God but an extension and arm of the vindictive ego.
- In most traditional religions retaliation is not presented as a sin or shameful. It is engaged in, shamelessly, by believers and their God. We notice that the moral imperative to eschew vengeance is not included in the Judeo-Christian Ten Commandments or in the Buddhist Precepts. We might say that revenge is the "forgotten sin."
- The self-help movement says hardly anything about the crucial value of letting go of retaliation for personal growth and healthy relating. "Retaliation" is the missing word in almost every self-help or spiritual book I have read.

Becoming aware of this "normal" orientation toward and justification of revenge may rightly scare us. We then design our behavior to assuage our fear: We mind our manners. We toe the line and remain on the lookout for what may trigger retaliation against us. We hold back our anger, or even our protest, however legitimate, in the political realm. We fear having our names in a file that may someday come to haunt us. Nonetheless, we see again how a dogged courage to be ourselves will be necessary if we are ever to maintain our integrity in a vengeful world.

Finally, with some dark humor, let's look at what the normalcy of retaliation might look like if was ever extended to an insane length. What if there were a school with this policy:

> We teach the necessity and validity of retaliation to our students from K-12. Please be advised that your child may occasionally come home with bruises or injuries, temporary or permanent, as a result of successful retribution by a fellow student. We do assure you, however, that we encourage students to gauge their retaliatory responses with absolute equity. Thus, if one student scratches the eye of another, we insist that the injured student scratch only one eye of the other student, not both.

We would certainly not sign our child up for that school. Yet we might not hesitate to tell our child: "If someone hits you, be sure to hit back." Likewise, if at eighteen the child we cherished and nurtured so tenderly were to be drafted to join a war of brutal retaliation, we might stand by without protest, since "patriotic duty calls." What will it take for us to confront the deep and enduring commitment to the legitimacy of retaliation that has been smuggled into us by a violence-driven society?

THE NORMALCY OF REVENGE
BEGAN LONG AGO

In Plato's *Crito,* Socrates says: "Let us take as the starting point of our discussion the assumption that it is never right to do wrong or to requite wrong with wrong, or when we suffer evil to defend ourselves by doing evil in return."[1] Socrates sees retaliation as a form of injustice. In his view, revenge harms the victim but harms the perpetrator even more. In Plato's *Republic*, we read: "For it has become apparent to us that it is never just to harm anyone. . . . It is better to suffer an injustice than to commit one."

Most ancient peoples did not follow Plato's view that taking revenge for an offense is worse for the soul than enduring someone's aggression toward us: His view is reflected in an old maxim: "Before you embark on a journey of revenge, be sure to dig two graves."

In ancient times, the common societal view was the one we see in Aristotle's *Nichomachean Ethics*: retaliation is required if we are ever to hold our head (ego) up high again after being harmed (the ego's entitlement to sovereignty).

Likewise, in his *Rhetoric*, Aristotle says: "Anger may be defined as an impulse, accompanied by pain, to a conspicuous revenge for a conspicuous slight directed without justification toward what concerns oneself or toward what concerns one's friends."[2] And elsewhere, "To take vengeance on one's enemies is nobler than to come to terms with them; for to retaliate is just."[3] He goes on to say that it is expedient and honorable to take revenge on enemies and not to choose reconciliation. Thus peacemaking, reconciling without vengeance, was considered losing face in the ancient world. It was considered shameful to let go of retaliation in favor of reconciliation and forgiveness. In Aristotle's view, to be injured, insulted, belittled, or treated with contempt requires, justifies, and sanctions revenge. The offended party can uphold its honor in society only by taking revenge. Thus, in ancient society, when Christians followed Jesus's teaching of forgoing revenge in reaction to a grievance, they were looked down on by their neighbors for having no sense of honor. It was thus doubly difficult to follow the spiritual practice of nonretaliation. Christians would not hit back *and* were blamed for not hitting back.

Ancient peoples believed it was equally healthy and appropriate to love one's friends and hate one's enemies. That belief was demonstrated by helping friends and harming enemies. The phrase "Love your enemies" was considered ludicrous and cowardly.

Roman law required retaliatory redress both for injury and insult. Ancient Jewish teachers and those in Jesus's time also fully approved of revenge. In the Hebrew Bible, God—like the Greek gods—defends his "honor" by exacting retribution:

> The Lord is a jealous and avenging God . . .
> The Lord takes vengeance on his foes and vents
> his wrath against his enemies (Nahum 1:2).

> The Lord has a day of vengeance, a year of retribution,
> to uphold Zion's cause (Isaiah 34:8).

Likewise, righteous people in the Bible seek revenge and yet remain righteous. Prophets call out to God to avenge his people, trusting that it is in his nature to do so:

> But you, Almighty Lord, who judge righteously and test
> the heart and mind, let me see your vengeance on them, for
> to you I have committed my cause (Jeremiah 11:20).

(Notice that righteousness—that is, justice—is the equivalent of vengeance.)

We also see divine vengeance splashed all over the first pages of the Bible. The backstory is that Lucifer had rebelled against God, who retaliated by hurling him into hell. To retaliate in turn, Lucifer, disguised as a serpent, arranges that God's newly created man and woman will rebel against him. God retaliates against

Adam and Eve by imposing penalties on them, including exile from Eden. We heard this story early in life and may never have questioned how it set the stage for our seeing revenge as normal, even necessary, and certainly not unethical. Most of us took retaliation in religious stories—as in myths and tales—in stride. We did not notice the absence of alternatives. That was a lacuna in our introduction to religion, passed on to us by those who received it from ancestors taught with the same lacuna.

In the Sermon on the Mount Jesus revokes the normalcy of retaliation in human behavior and dubs it shameful. He calls peacemaking honorable: "Be reconciled with your brother" (Matthew 5:24). Thus, he reverses the conventional view of the time and of the previous centuries. Jesus's recommendation is not to defend one's honor, maintain one's reputation, or maintain a shiny image in the eyes of the public, as Aristotle recommends. Jesus thereby presents quite a subversive teaching: in a world in which honor and reputation are primary, he proposes living by a standard that disregards those concerns altogether. Any capital gained by looking good becomes disposable income.

Turning to medieval theology, St. Thomas Aquinas proposes that vengeance can't be essentially evil or unlawful, since God engages in it. He quotes Deuteronomy 32:35: "Vengeance is mine says the Lord; I will repay." It is only vengeance taken by individuals that is unlawful. Yet St. Thomas also says that if an avenger's intention is to do good, vengeance is acceptable. An example he gives is that our retribution might be a deterrent to further violence. It might be a wake-up call that teaches the offender to recognize his wrongs and encourage him to make amends. Thus, in Aquinas's perspective, God can retaliate but we can do so only in very limited circumstances. Regarding penal cases in court and the meting out of punishment, he quotes Romans 13:4 to show the legitimacy of vengeance by lawful authorities, since they are "God's ministers, agents of wrath to bring punishment on evildoers." It's hard to read "God is love" in such a fulmination.

WHERE RETALIATION MAY HIDE

The frequency of retaliatory responses from us and others also makes it seem normal. A vindictive reaction to an insult or injury is automatic and involuntary in most of us. Sometimes it is calculated, but sometimes it is instantaneous. To de-normalize retaliation will take careful and constant vigilance over our attitudes, choices, and actions. Vengeance is an expert at hiding, especially from ourselves. Normalcy thrives on what is unnoticed. The first step on the path to letting go of retaliating is noticing all the little ways we do it.

Here is an example of how retaliation can happen in a second and be so subtle that we don't realize we are engaging in it. Someone snubs us and we immediately say: "To hell with her!" We then put on a show of not caring that the person snubbed us. Even the turning away on our part is a form of retaliation. We are trying to get back at the offender by making sure she understands that her snub is unimportant to us, that she can't get our goat. Retaliation often has the goal of showing offenders that they are utterly impotent to make any impact on us, the invulnerable ones.

Most of us are not skilled at examining our motives carefully. We think, "He tried to get ahead of me in line. I hung back and let him do that. I showed that I am bigger than he is. I am also being humble and gracious." But actually, we were trying to show him up, to shame him for his discourtesy. We were teaching him a lesson. We may someday notice that retaliation endorses our own arrogance and insistence on one-upmanship, which is another word for ego grandiosity.

Another subtle, usually unnoticed example of retaliation is fooling people who think they are fooling us: "She thought she was getting away with cheating or harming me, but by hook or by crook I ultimately benefited." We may have noticed that the harlequinesque humor in cartoons is often based on retaliation. Road Runner always wins, to the disgruntlement of Wile E. Coyote, who is so sure he will be the successful retaliator. Both retaliate in every scene, though Road Runner is the expert at it. Are we at the cartoon level of relating when we exact revenge?

We might also deny our own vengefulness by getting someone else to be the bad guy. For instance, we hire a lawyer known to be a predatory barracuda to carry out what we want to be a nasty divorce. A religious example is in the traditional view that God recruited Lucifer to carry out his punitive retaliation against sinners. He created a brutal warehouse, hell, in which it could be thoroughly carried out. God has the devil make sure the torments last forever, with no chance for repentance or the payment of debt. What part of the heartless ego came up with that scenario?

WHAT LOOKS NORMAL

Here is a list of aggressive behaviors that are often retaliatory. Retaliation seems normal when it is commonly accepted or goes unnamed. We also notice that they sometimes occur between people who are in a love-hate relationship:

- "Gotcha!" (the ego's favorite word).
- Excluding in any of the following forms: ghosting (sudden unexplained silence), ostracizing, boycotting, snubbing, giving someone the cold shoulder, pouting, holding a grudge, using the silent treatment, spitefully unfriending someone on social media, deliberately seducing someone and then withholding romantic contact.
- Showing contempt by belittling, mocking, bad-mouthing, insulting, digs, barbs, put-downs, disrespect, demeaning, defaming, slandering, libeling, shaming, judging, criticizing, making fun of or humiliating, causing someone to lose face in front

of others, besmirching someone's reputation, rudeness, oppositional defiance (within a family or at work), vulgar or biased remarks—e.g., racist comments or jokes—profiling that leads to aggression.

- Being directly or passively aggressive, being abusive in any way, including playing practical jokes with a mean edge, being spiteful, snarky, bullying, teasing, weaponizing sex, gunning for someone who rejected us, showing ill will, intimidation, picking someone up on every little thing, road rage, using social media to cause harm to or shame someone, using sarcasm or comebacks to cause shame or pain, traumatizing, tricking, deliberately doing what annoys the other person, engaging in physical, emotional, spiritual, or sexual harm.

- Holding onto prejudices that lead to vengeful actions—e.g., Christians who believe that Jews killed Christ and justify their anti-Semitism.

- Preemptive retaliation—"I'll beat him to the punch!"

- Retribution as aggression: sometimes the aggression toward us takes the form of retribution from someone who is angry at us based on actions of ours that had full integrity, e.g., we were only doing our job but caused them embarrassment or loss.

- Scolding someone for being inadequate, for being late, for forgetting to fulfill a commitment when we believe those behaviors were insulting to or inconsiderate toward us. Here our indignant ego uses reprimand as retribution.

- Wishing someone's defeat or hardship, feeling schadenfreude, rejoicing over others' distress, gloating over or being glad about the defeat or hardship of those we don't like or who harmed us.

- Teasing or harming pets.

- Displacing aggression—e.g., the boss upbraids us and we then pass the aggression along by scolding our partner or children.

- Still holding rancor against our parents for how they treated us in childhood.

- Disinheriting our offspring because of their behavior or choices.
- Parents keeping their children away from grandparents to spite them.
- Sometimes committing suicide includes an element of revenge against one's survivors, a last act of payback.
- Church authorities refusing Communion to politicians who support a woman's right to an abortion or refusing burial in "consecrated ground" to a person who committed suicide.

SOUND BITES

Retaliatory sentiments are often spoken silently in our minds, and sometimes aloud. We react to people and events with hostility and aggression. We might hear ourselves think or say any of the following statements and not recognize them as retaliation.

- "I asked the person in authority for the permission I wanted. She refused to give it to me. I asked elsewhere and got it. Then, for spite, I made sure she saw that I now had it. I showed her she could not stop me from getting what I wanted."
- "I was treated less than courteously at a restaurant, so I won't go back there. I post a negative online review in order to get even." (A review meant to call the manager's attention to inadequate service and help others make an informed decision about going to that restaurant is, of course, not retaliatory.)
- "I am so glad that someone finally called you on the carpet!"
- "I won't make concessions since you haven't."
- "I will sue you big-time for what you have done to me." (A lawyer is sometimes used for revenge purposes.)
- "I owe you money, but I am angry at you so I will make you wait for payment or not pay you at all."
- "I don't have what I want (for example, a possession, a career position, or an intimate relationship). Motivated by envy,

I hope it does not work out for people who do have what I lack and crave."

- "I show the people who tried to ruin my life that I am better off in my new life away from them." (They see that they were not successful in defeating me after all.)
- "I show the person who rejected me that the rejection has not fazed me." An example is replying to a rejecting email with a thumbs-up emoji.
- "I wish her dead" or "I am glad she died."
- "He offended me long ago and I still hate him."
- "She never said she was sorry, so I want nothing more to do with her."
- "I saw your ex and she looks wonderful, best I have ever seen her, so happy!"
- "I am glad the states that don't support legislation I favor will lose federal funding." (Here both we and Washington collude in retaliation.)

We notice in all of the above listings that retaliation cancels our opportunity to show compassion. Retaliating is dangerous to spiritual growth.

Notice the word "show" in some of the above examples. Whenever we are righteously trying to show something to someone who hurt our feelings we have to examine our motive to see if it is actually a form of patronizing with a spiteful intent. We also notice in this list that the issue of a power differential comes up almost every time: "I have the power now and you don't," or "I had it and you took it and now I got it back," or "I made it clear that you don't have, or never have had, power."

Finally, in a slightly humorous vein, a person may feel slighted or insulted and, as payback, do something that shows the other person up: "My well-to-do colleague invited me to dinner and served beans and hot dogs. I, who make less than he does, invited him to dinner a month later and served leg of lamb with all the trimmings." I might then pride myself and justify my behavior as "positive" retaliation.

SECRET MOTIVES

Our belief that we have good reasons for retaliation also contributes to the sense of its normalcy. We can summarize our possible motivations for revenge: to right a wrong, to heal our bruised ego, to deter others from causing further harm, to evince guilt or shame from the transgressor, to restore or cause a balance of power, to express righteous anger, to teach the other a lesson, and to make us feel good—or great—again. But sometimes there is a hidden psychological motivation, conscious or unconscious, when we gather our weapons from the arsenal of revenge. The weapons can be used to support a denial that we are actually retaliating. Let's ponder four escape hatches we might use to make our behavior seem normal, ordinary, and logical when there is a lot more behind it. All of them serve to establish the normalcy of retaliation.

1. We May Retaliate to Circumvent Life's Givens of Unfairness or Betrayal

A common fuel for revenge is believing that this is or has to be a just world. We may then find ourselves battling the implacable givens of unfairness and betrayals that are part of every human life. The vindictive ego believes itself entitled to an exemption from such unwelcome truths.

Simply righting a wrong is not the whole picture in the view-finder of an inflated ego. We also feel personally entitled to be treated justly and kindly. In other words, the givens of life don't apply to us, our superior ego tells us we are excused from them. This is self-favoritism that supports and perpetuates what we consider our privileged status. We refuse to say yes to the fact of disappointment, betrayal, hurt, and hate—the sufferings in any human life. We imagine we deserve a special dispensation, immunity from what applies only to all those other people. We think, "Bad things are not supposed to happen me. So I will take my indignation out on those who have been unfair toward me."

The vindictive ego attempts to duck the given of suffering and grief by taking revenge. We deny the fact that suffering is a necessary ingredient of life. And what is worse, we take our indignation out on someone else. Our ego entitlement convinces us we have full permission to harm those who harmed us. Then the fact of unfairness in every human life truly does not apply to us! We deserve better. Likewise, our revenge gives our offenders what they deserve.

Let's take a look at the word *deserve*. It comes from the Latin *deservire*, which is based on the word for serving others. The connotation is "You have served me well, so you are entitled to a reward." We notice the elitist, top-down style embedded in that concept of *deserve*. In the dualistic ego world of tit-for-tat, people deserve punishment if they offend us, and a reward if they please us. We might then believe that to give someone "what he deserves" or "what's coming to him" for his offense is not really retaliating but only just desserts. In the spiritually aware world of higher consciousness, reward and punishment do not find quarter. We appreciate those who are kind to us and we speak up with compassionate communication to those who offend us. We do this not with spite but with kindliness.

On a humorous note, we might add that the generous spirit of unconditional deservingness will sound like the words of the charming dodo bird in *Alice in Wonderland*: "Everybody has won and all must have prizes." That can happen when we prize all our fellow humans, the style of the loving-kindness practice in Buddhism and the practice of *agape*, selfless love in humanist or religious traditions.

2. We May Retaliate to Avoid
the Full Feeling of Grief

Retaliation evades grief and dialogue in favor of inflicting suffering on the one who inflicted it on us. It is not meant to repair a relationship but to spite the offender. When we trespass against the person who trespassed against us, we are offloading our suffering. We are opting to reduce the weight of our own burden of pain by getting the perpetrator to carry some of its load or all of it.

When we want to avoid messy feelings in grief, we may believe that getting even is our best way out. Yet it turns out to be a booby prize, since most forms of flight also distance us from true relating. Intimacy thrives on openness and vulnerability. Revenge sets all bonds asunder.

Sadness is the appropriate response to being offended by someone. We may, however, hold back our tears because we see it as a sign of weakness. We also avoid an assertion of healthy anger, which is appropriate to any offense, betrayal, or hurt. Likewise, we are afraid to engage in the fourfold mindful practice: experiencing our grief, saying "Ouch!," opening a dialogue, and including the other in our loving-kindness practice, even if it is simply feeling goodwill toward the person. We know all that might make our ego too vulnerable. We might prefer to show what feels like strength—by getting even.

We also keep in mind that in a workplace, or in any interaction with an authority figure, all bets may be off. Our practice works only when we are safe to engage in it. A threatening power differential may not permit us to speak up. This caution applies to all the recommendations to speak up throughout this book.

In Shakespeare's *Troilus and Cressida*, we hear: "Hope of revenge shall hide our inward woe."[4] Thus revenge may serve as a surrogate for grief. Our inflated and indignant ego tells us we don't have to be sad that we have been harmed, betrayed, insulted, disrespected. We can get back at the one who hurt us. We can turn our righteous rage and its accompanying grief into retribution, which is a skewed form of reciprocity. We might also use other forms of avoidance. In postwar Germany, which was ripe for grief, perhaps the avoidance took the form of an intense focus on rebuilding the bombed-out edifices: *rebuilding* shall hide our inward woe. We can ask ourselves what forms our own avoidance of grief may be taking? What are our personal stand-ins for grief?

The healthy response to a hurt or offense will, of course, have to include assertiveness skills: we show our anger, but without aggression. This is the opposite of the old advice: "Don't get mad, get even!" We are honest enough to acknowledge our fear to ourselves and are careful not to override it with acting as if we were invulnerable. We don't try to come across as intimidating. We remind ourselves that healthy anger is not an act of aggression; it is a feeling we communicate nonviolently.

Our desire to get back at someone can sometimes be used to show us what we need to confront in ourselves. Retaliation is tricky, since as a cover-up it has an element of self-deception. Troilus did not look deeply enough into his statement to realize a truth about himself: "I fear my own feelings; I fear my grief."

When we feel hurt by what someone has done to us and we dodge our grief, we may cheer ourselves up by a plan to retaliate. We then feel an instant sense of empowerment. We were hurt and disempowered by how we were wronged. We feel suddenly strong because we have come up with a plan to right the wrong. We can get the offender without having to feel the grief about what they did to us. We believe we have moved from victim to hero, though we have only become a persecutor. In other words, we have ourselves become the aggressors, and we remain in a victim mindset by engaging in retaliation. We can move from being a victim of abuse to becoming a reconciler when we practice going beyond retaliation. We then declare: I am not a victim of an injury when

I practice nonviolence, forgiveness, and loving-kindness. I am a survivor of it and I am a victor over it. I am also a new person altogether.

Another way we might sidestep expressing our grief is by engaging in projective identification: I don't want to feel this pain so I will get you to feel it, and visibly too. I then see my feeling in you rather than feel it in myself. I believe it is not my feeling but yours.

Projective identification of what we reckon to be negative feelings is a form of retaliation and is always an offloading: She is often late for our meetups and I find it irritating. To get back at her, I will arrive late to a meeting that is important to her. I will then see the irritation on her face when I show up late. We believe that our retaliation has worked perfectly. We got back at her for being late. We believe the projective identification has worked. We see our own anger on her face without ever having to let on that we have been angry all this time. And it all seems normal and fully justified—exactly what we want vengeance to feel like.

Retaliation is always a circumvention, though it may seem to be a direct hit. In the realm of transference, for example, a form of projection, adults who were controlled or criticized by a parent may take out their anger on people in their present life. Innocent bystanders may now be paying the price for what an abusive parent did decades ago. Another common example is problems with authority figures, including those at work. We won't fulfill their orders or do it their way. That may be our way of retaliating against any authority, but really it is aimed at all the people, family members and others, who inhibited or restrained us in our past. They humiliated us and now we can get back at anyone in the archetype, role, or category that they represent.

We might also be engaging in the same anachronistic payback toward an intimate partner. Darren was controlled and engulfed in childhood by his mother. He was in her power until he left home but still feels he is in her grasp. Darren, even now as a married man, does not dare show aggressive feelings toward his mom and transfers his rage onto his wife. He is getting back at his mother through her. She does not guess she is a stand-in, nor does Darren. Someday if he notices what he has been up to, apologizes and works on his mother issues, the transference will cease as a welcome result.

Most people would not connect the dots and see a displacement from past to present. This is why psychologically aware people keep examining their behavior to look for where revenge may be lurking. Retaliation has been directly connected to survival since prehistoric times, so it does not exit us descendants easily.

3. We May Retaliate Out of Envy

Most of us are ashamed to show that we are envious. We don't want to be seen as one-down or lacking, which is what envy implies. Instead, we turn envy into retaliation but do not call it that or let anyone know that is what we are up to. We might find ways to harm others just because they have more money, possessions, or status than we do.

The definition of envy is painful or resentful awareness of an advantage enjoyed by another and a desire to possess the same advantage. St. Thomas Aquinas, in his *Summa Theologica*, defined envy, one of the seven deadly sins, as "sorrow at another's good." He describes love as "willing the good" for the other. St. Paul wrote: "Rejoice with those who rejoice; weep with those who weep" (Romans 12:15). In Buddhism, too, a quality of an enlightened person is joy, not envy, at the success or happiness of others. Likewise, Buddhist teachings include compassion for those who suffer.

Admiration is the healthy response to seeing something in others that we appreciate, honor, or are impressed by. Envy is the negative shadow side of admiration: people who deserve esteem are seen as rivals. When we admire someone we say: "I am impressed with you or with what you have accomplished." In admiration we show esteem and may also want to emulate those we appreciate. We celebrate their achievement or good fortune.

Envy is about comparing. We begrudge others their success or happiness:

"You shouldn't have it, I should have it."
"If I can't have it, neither should you."
"They don't deserve what they have since I don't get to have it."

None of these three statements may seem to us like retaliation, but rather like a righteous response to unfairness. We can see how easily envy masks our vengeful thoughts, plans, and actions. Recently a friend told me that he sometimes finds the electric charger of his Tesla unhooked when he returns to it. He noticed that the Toyotas and Fords are still plugged in. Another friend, a mechanic who works mainly on Porsches, said he has to keep the parking area closed at night because people walking by have sometimes keyed just the Porsches. How mean-spirited is a belief like this: "If I can't have it neither should you."

One final point: sibling rivalry is certainly an example of envy. "When Joseph's brothers saw that their father loved him more than all his other sons, they hated him" (Genesis 37:4). In that instance envy led to hate of a brother and eventually to a vengeful plan, not acted out, to kill him. Instead, they sold him into slavery. The brothers would not have called this payback, but rather Joseph's getting his just desserts for his privileged—envied—position in the family. Joseph forgave his brothers, which is the spiritual response to envy-driven aggression and a move toward healing the harm and division it can cause. Joseph also noticed that what the brothers meant to be evil had been turned into good. That happens in forgiveness, not in vengeance. When envy-driven retaliation is named rather than denied, it can lead to a transformation of all parties—in the Bible story, all twelve brothers. Revenge is returning evil for evil; forgiveness is returning love for evil. Revenge deforms; forgiveness transforms.

THE MYSTERY OF EVIL

This chapter began with Hannah Arendt's commentary on the banality of evil. Let's end the chapter with an exploration of what is meant by evil. We open our discussion with a powerful statement from Father Pedro Arrupe, SJ, former head of the Jesuit order, in his 1973 Address to Graduates of Jesuit Schools in Europe:

> Most of us would be relatively good in a good world. What is difficult is to be good in an evil world, where the egoism of others and the egoism built into the institutions of society attack us and threaten to annihilate us.
>
> Under such conditions, the only possible reaction would seem to be to oppose evil with evil, egoism with egoism, hate with hate; in short, to annihilate the aggressor with his own weapons. But is it not precisely thus that evil conquers us most thoroughly? For then, not only does it damage us exteriorly, it perverts our very heart. . . . Evil is overcome only by good, hate by love, egoism by generosity. It is thus that we must sow justice in our world. To be just, it is not enough to refrain from injustice. One must go further and refuse to play its game, substituting love for self-interest as the driving force of society.[5]

Evil is a mystery. But we can say something about the elements of an evil act:

- We intend and do grave harm.
- Our action involves a serious matter.
- We act with malice.

- We are fully aware that what we are doing is wrong.
- We are acting with the full consent of our will—that is, voluntarily.

An example of an evil act is murder in the first degree: someone wills an evil effect—that is, the criminal death of the victim, with no mitigating circumstances and with full understanding that murder is wrong. (Psychopaths have an organic deficit of empathy, a lack of conscience, so the question of choice becomes moot.)

Not even a good end justifies an evil means, but when evil happens anyway, good can sometimes come of it, though this does not justify evil choices.

Sometimes we choose the cause that leads to a harmful end while not deliberately willing that effect. An alcoholic husband knows he will most likely strike his wife and children if he drinks too much. He then is actually choosing to be abusive when he engages in excessive drinking.

Sometimes evil is willed in both the cause and effect. For instance, the advertising committee members of a tobacco company vote to aim advertisements at teenage children while knowing that vaping and smoking will definitely harm their health, be likely to lead to addiction, and possibly end in death. Unlike premeditated murder, the tobacco company willfully reaches out to teens, but not intentionally to cause the possible lethal effect—that is, cancer. Yet tobacco companies know of the deleterious effects of their products, so they have willed evil in cause and effect. In this instance, intentional greed—a malicious intent—is the motivation.

Some acts can be harmful, but we are not responsible for any resulting evil. For instance, we know that driving a car causes harm to the environment, but we are not maliciously intending that result or seeking personal gain. So evil in this instance cannot be imputed to the driver, but the driver is doing harm. Likewise, killing in self-defense or to protect others from being killed is doing harm, but it is not an evil in itself. All evil is harmful, but not all that is harmful is evil.

Evil is a quality of a human act. People perpetrate evil acts. Acts are evil, but people are not. At the same time, some people give themselves over to evil deeds so often and so fully that they become possessed by evil and so are considered evil by society—for example, Hitler or Stalin. Such people don't consider their evil deeds to be wrong, only necessary. They normalize evil in their own minds but are still culpable. In the plays of Shakespeare, for instance, Macbeth and Iago normalized the evil that possessed them, but Laertes and Othello only did evil things.

Evil is not only a quality of an individual act but can also be systemic. It exists in corporate, political, and religious institutions that perpetuate injustice, abuse, greed, and war. Systemic evil exists in most of society's institutions. In recent years, we have seen the corrupt underbelly of one venerated institution after another. All institutions, like all people, have a shadow side: a life-, justice-, and freedom-negating agenda. Whistle-blowers are the assisting forces in the human community who turn the spotlight on them and on ourselves.

In Buddhism we are warned of three poisons that prevent enlightenment: greed, hate, and ignorance. All three can pave the way to retaliatory behavior. In greed, we want more and more and may be vengeful toward those we envy for having it. We retaliate more and more against those we hate. We retaliate out of ignorance of our interconnectedness as humans, thinking we have a separate existence or that our life is worth more than the lives of others. Notice the varied uses of the word "more" in the above description of the three poisons. Pursuing each "more" leads to winding up with less. Indeed, pursuing recrimination is precisely about a life of less: less generosity, less love, less connection.

There are many ways to respond to evil. Three stand out: passivity, violent resistance, or nonviolent resistance. What is called the reptilian brain—that is, our brain center of primitive, aggressive, uncivilized impulses—supports the first two options. The third way is militant nonviolence. This is not passivity or obsequious submission, but resolute opposition to evil using peaceful means—what Martin Luther King Jr. often called "soul force" and what Gandhi called "truth force."

Nonviolence is not a goal but a virtue, a habit, an ethical choice in the face of evil and aggression. Its only purpose is the peace and survival of all concerned. It is not a strategy to win but to *win over* others to the disarming arts of fruitful relating. We act this way in our relationships whether others show loving-kindness to us or even thank us for it. Faithfulness to our own standard of love is so satisfying that recognition by or thanks from others is no longer a priority. Now even our political purposes have become enlightened. The old lyrics "We shall overcome someday" mean that we shall overcome injustice, war, and hate, not that we will show the officials who support them how wrong they are. This is what a new way of living looks like.

Evil easily wins approval when it is motivated by what we judge to be a positive purpose or when it offers the possibility of a beneficial outcome. In such instances, we may believe that a good intention can justify an evil result. Of course, good intentions do not justify evil. As it is said, the road to hell is paved with good intentions. But the irony is that sometimes evil leads to an unexpected good, as in the story of Joseph and his brothers. Friedrich Nietzsche in *Human, All Too Human* states: "Such evil and painful incidents belong to the history of the great emancipation."[6]

FIVE

Why We Punish

PUNISHMENT IS THE inflicting of pain or loss as retribution for an offense. In a legal procedure, punishment is meted out for three main reasons: to correct or reform, to redress a wrong, or to deter others who might become similar offenders. Punishment by a legal authority has traditionally included any of the following elements:

- a loss of freedom, as in jail time
- a loss of money, as in payments of fines
- undergoing a hardship, as in labor or community-service obligations
- execution

Appropriate punishment is a curb on inordinate revenge. Jail time has a termination date. A fine is stated as a one-time specific amount. Hard labor or community service happen within stated limits. All three can lead to a restoration of the criminal to society. Execution is retributive only and not in keeping with restorative justice or mature spiritual consciousness.

In retaliation we may perpetrate the same injury on to the other as was done to us. We might also do something different from that which was done to us, but usually with equal impact or purpose. In any way the retaliation happens, the intention is the same: to harm or hurt. Punishment may not be retaliatory in that sense. A parent who punishes a child, for instance, does not intend to hurt but to correct. A mother whose son has insulted her punishes by grounding him, not by insulting him back. In a legal procedure the court punishes our crime of robbery by sending us to jail or fining us. It does not retaliate in kind by robbing us. Retaliation from one person to another is geared to target the individual, whereas in a court sentence the punishment follows the same standard for all offenders. All the above, of course, only happens when justice prevails in a society.

Punishment as lockup in an overcrowded warehousing prison is retaliatory. Prison programs that are based entirely on such punishment have higher rates of recidivism than those based on rehabilitation. The prisoners do not learn how to integrate themselves back into society. Punishment as a program of rehabilitation is not retaliatory but restorative. The transgressor is restored to the community and readied to participate in society as a law-abiding citizen. Prison systems such as the humanistic ones in Norway stand out because they focus on how a prisoner can ultimately become civic-minded and a good neighbor. The recidivism rate in Norway is as low as 20 percent. The incarcerated there are treated as people in recovery who can learn life skills that will help them toward rehabilitation. This is a restorative rather than retributive style of justice.

There are other differences between personal revenge and legal punishment. For instance, in fair adjudication the punishment is meant to fit the crime. In revenge the avenger feels he has the right to overdo it. Personal revenge often includes lawlessness and irrationality. Retaliatory punishment by a legitimate authority is carried out in a well-ordered way. It is not scattershot, as may happen in person-to-person revenge.

The state attempts to normalize capital punishment by means of an orderly ritual: the condemned chooses a last meal, the minister reads prayers as he accompanies the criminal to the gallows, the condemned person is given an opportunity for any last words. The execution is carried out in a dispassionate manner in the presence of official silent witnesses.

In 1945, in the Palace of Justice at Nuremberg, Germany, Justice Robert H. Jackson, chief counsel for the United States, said: "That four great nations, flushed with victory and stung with injury stay the hand of vengeance and voluntarily submit their captive enemies to the judgment of the law is one of the most significant tributes that Power has ever paid to Reason."[1] The rule of law does indeed combine power and reason. Perhaps Justice Jackson did not recognize that hanging the criminals was a form of vengeance. The normalcy of the condemned men's evil was followed by the normalcy of revenge.

Seeking an alternative option, let's listen to the Holocaust survivor Elie Weisel in his book *One Generation After*: "Rejected by mankind, the condemned do not go so far as to reject it in turn. Their faith in history remains unshaken. . . . They do not despair. . . . The victims elect to become witnesses."[2] He shows us the elements of letting go of retaliation: faith in the positive arc of human history and in human redeemability, hope in the fact that humans do not have to retaliate, trust that we can commit ourselves to be witnesses to injustice, after which we are in a position to call it out, protest it, and take nonviolent action to end it.

PUNISHMENT IN CHILDHOOD

We might punish a child for an infraction or for breaking house rules by sending her to her room. In such instances, we want to teach socialization: correct, not harm. In this regard, we also keep in mind that isolating a child has been shown to be an unskillful way to teach a lesson. Dialogue and making a plan together for redress seems more effective than isolation as a form of correction. Some parents punish to correct. Abusive parents punish to exact retribution. We can ask ourselves which kind of punishment our parents used on us, whether it was from love and corrective or from malice and vindictive. We might ask ourselves how our own experience in childhood has affected our behavior in relationships or in child-rearing now.

THE SIX EDITORS

Many of us were taught that following what authority figures deem acceptable behavior leads to safety and security. We might have been punished in early life if we made unacceptable choices, showed certain personality traits, did not adhere to societal or family conventions, had beliefs that were considered extreme, or engaged in behaviors that were marginal in any way. We noticed we had to watch our step and do what the authorities wanted us to do, otherwise we might be punished or, worse, abandoned. This may have been when we first saw that a connection could be broken, at our peril, if we dared upset others by being ourselves.

Following up on this last sentence, as an aside, I am recalling this note at the beginning of some films presented on television: "This film has been formatted to fit your screen." I see that announcement as a metaphor. Six spheres of influence and formatting stand out: family, religion (or any source of moral teaching), school, peers, media (both social media and entertainment), and society. It is up to us conscious adults to assess the contributions of these "editors" and decide which ones to live by and which to toss. In accord with our theme, we particularly notice how much we bought into their recommendations on loving-kindness and retaliation.

I see hope in these words of Stephen Batchelor in *Buddhism Without Beliefs*: "Individuation is a process of recovering personal authority through freeing ourselves from the constraints of collectively held belief systems."[3] So becoming me will take showing my authentic feelings, needs, wishes, and values—a big challenge when safety has always meant obedience.

On a humorous note, the phrase "fit your screen" means made smaller to fit others' requirements. I was brought up in New Haven, called "the elm city." I am elm, but am I bonsai?

THE PUNITIVE BARB

Retaliation usually includes an element of punishment, as is clear in any of these common phrases:

"Boy, will they be sorry! I'll show them! They will pay for this. They will get what's coming to them. I'll get back at them. I won't forget this! I'll hold this against them for a long time. I'll get them for this. They will never hear the end of this. I'll fix their wagon. I will teach them a lesson. They won't get away with this. I will even the score. Now they get a taste of their own medicine! He got what he deserved. I showed him who's boss. He will live to regret this."

"He did this to me, so I will do the same to him. He did not do this for me, so I won't do that for him. I am holding it against him and waiting for my chance at payback."

"I did her a favor and she did not return the favor. I will do no more favors for her, or I will find other ways to get back at her."

"It's my way or the highway."

"I will hit him where it hurts, his pocketbook. I know just where to put the knife in."

"I will boycott them for still being friendly toward the person who hurt me."

"He did not take my side, so I want no more to do with him."

"I know she wants it, so for spite I won't give it to her."

"I will pay them back for rebuffing or rejecting me."

"I will distribute 'revenge porn' online to embarrass and shame him" (an illegal act).

"In a relationship, I am spoiling for a fight." (The "spoiling" certainly describes what we will be doing to our connection with the other person.)

"We are on the outs now, so I am not going to help him in his recent crisis."

"I am glad he was unkind to me because now I really have a reason to be angry, and that gives me the right to retaliate."

"You don't seem to like my way of doing this for you, so go find someone else to do it" (rather than discussing the problem and staying with the original arrangement).

"You are a micromanager, so I will procrastinate doing the job you asked me to do in order to frustrate and annoy you."

"I won't give you the satisfaction of seeing that you got to me!"

"Now that I got back at you, the joke is on you. I got the last laugh." (That was not actually a laugh but a payback.)

"God punished you [and I am glad]!"

All these statements are examples of aggression that are both retaliatory and punitive. Indeed, a lack of assertiveness in asking for a dialogue is often followed by aggressiveness, especially passive-aggressiveness.

The will to punish is not consistent with love. Punishment is a top-down rebuke rather than a form of restoring harmony by negotiation, amends, forgiveness, and reconciliation. In a truly respectful bond we look together for ways to restore mutuality, beginning with nonviolent communication of our feelings. An "Ouch!" can open into reconciliation. Retaliation closes down that opportunity.

We can always ask for or name accountability, which makes no comment on the character of the accused person. Blame assigns guilt with disapproval, censure, reproach, condemnation, and a reviling of the person's character. In mature spiritual consciousness no one is to blame or deserves punishment, though everyone is accountable and can make amends or compensation. In forgiveness we fully let go of blame while remaining conscious of accountability. In other words, we *neither excuse nor condemn* our offenders. Nor as adults will we excuse or continue to blame our parents for how they may have mistreated us in childhood. Forgiveness works in all directions, healing past, present, and future too. It is also a major part of the path to being an adult.

Sometimes revenge by the wronged people facilitates their forgiveness of the provoking person because, to them, justice seems to have been done. This is, of course, punitive justice, not restorative justice that generates equity through nonviolent communication. The "forgiveness" is highly conditioned and is not the style of virtue or authenticity.

Let's look more closely at the distinction between retributive and restorative justice. Revenge is fueled by a compulsion to engage in payback. Revenge is retributive damage, the opposite of restorative justice. The former breaks connection while the latter is about coming up with a plan to reconcile and bring all concerned back to an experience of community. Restorative justice can include compensation, amends, repentance, and skillful discourse between offender and victim. We take part in it. In retributive justice a sentence is pronounced on us. We become the objects who now must pay back society.

Restorative justice promotes repairing the damage caused by an offense. It is not limited to courts; it is a style of behavior that can help any of us in times of conflict or aggression. This form of justice will include facilitating reconciliation between the wrongdoer and the victim if possible. Retributive punishment is meant to harm, not to reform, to reject, not to restore. It does not acknowledge the value of human solidarity—what we are going for in a spiritual practice.

SANCTION AND EXCLUSION

We can distinguish vengeance from natural consequences or strong forms of protest. Sanctions placed on one or more nations against another nation are not retaliatory. They are communications and consequences meant to halt or intervene on further injustices. An economic penalty against a nation that disregards international law is an example. Another international example is responding to tariffs with tariffs. That is not revenge, a move to escalate conflict, but an attempt to evince a change or a reversal. Sanctions usually follow unsuccessful diplomatic attempts to dissuade the offending nation from its aggressive actions. The fact that sanctions will be lifted as soon as the injustices end shows that the penalties are meant to be remedial, not retributive. They are not meant to be divisive or competitive but are imposed to foster the common good, public safety, and security.

What about exiling, excluding, or ostracizing in societal or personal relationships? One of the members of a weekly card game is caught cheating and the group does not allow him back. The group is not retaliating, only excluding someone who refuses to play by the rules. The cheating member brought this consequence onto himself.

An offender, within a community, commits an egregious crime against a fellow member. He admits his guilt, but the court, based on a technicality, exonerates him. The community confronts the criminal and banishes him. This is not retaliation. It is a legitimate chastisement in the form of a non-physically harming exclusion from an offended society. In this instance, there is no possibility of rejoining the community later, even when the offender shows compunction. Yet it is still appropriate castigation and not retaliation since the community does not want to take him back as a member, which is their right, while wishing him no harm—that is, without intending or showing malice. Of course, if many years later the miscreant reapplies for admission, the community can take another look. Justice, seasoned with mercy, requires such a look. In many states a convicted felon cannot vote. But the criminal's right to vote is restored once his sentence is served.

To excommunicate someone from a religious community, especially a cult, is not retaliation when the punishment is meant to encourage the offender to repent and be reconciled with the community. Let's look at this advice from St. Paul: "If anyone does not obey our word in this epistle, note that person and do not keep company with him, that he may be ashamed" (2 Thessalonians 3:14). If the shame is meant to inflict trauma, the ostracizing is retaliatory. If it is meant to be a catalyst to repentance—that is, to a positive change—it can be a legitimate reprimand. (We note that not obeying the word of a teacher does not constitute a reason for ostracizing in today's free world.)

In personal relationships, we may decide to cease further contact with someone we no longer like or with whom we no longer have anything in common. That separation is not retaliatory as long as it does not include ghosting and we tell the other about our decision in a kind way. In instances in which we haven't been hearing from the other person anyway, we can let the relationship drift off without comment on our part. However, if we are hurtful or damaging to that person or try to ruin his or her reputation, then our ostracizing is retaliatory. Motive makes the difference.

OUR NEED FOR A HELL

Holding on to a belief in hell as punishment by means of eternal torture—usually in reference to other people, not to ourselves—is an intention to have revenge exacted beyond the grave. When the ego can't retaliate enough, it feels entitled to have its revenge handled by an avenging God who is never fully propitiated. The inflated ego is, in that instance, the real name of the Almighty.

As we saw, punishment can have a positive dimension. It can be a form of correction and restoration. In mature religious consciousness, God is, as Thomas Merton said, "mercy upon mercy" and therefore completely free of vengeful motivations. In the Orthodox tradition, St. Isaac of Syria in the seventh century also realized this and wrote: "God chastises with love, not for the sake of revenge . . . but in seeking to make whole his image. . . . This is the aim of love. Love's chastisement is for correction, but does not aim at retribution."[4] Likewise, in the Western mystic tradition, we see a similar view. Julian of Norwich, in *Revelations of Divine Love*, describes a vision in which she sees an alternative to the traditional teaching on hell: "I understood that sinners are worthy sometime of blame and wrath; but these two could I not see in God."[5]

In more modern times, St. Thérèse of Lisieux, in an 1897 letter to Father Adolphe Roulland, speaks in the same vein:

That, my Brother, is what I think of the justice of the good God, my way is entirely one of trust and love, I do not understand the souls who are afraid of such a tender Friend.[6]

St. Augustine, in a letter to Bishop Januarius, wrote: "This, then, is our desire that we bring before Your Reverence. . . . First, that if possible, you confer peacefully with your bishops in order that the error itself may be destroyed, not the human beings in whom it is found, that human beings not be punished, but corrected."[7]

We see a harsh alternative response in the Book of Revelation: "When he opened the fifth seal, I saw under the altar the souls of those who had been slain because of the word of God and the testimony they had maintained. They called out in a loud voice, 'How long, Sovereign Lord, holy and true, until you judge the inhabitants of the earth and avenge our blood?'" (6:9–10). The souls speaking in this passage were never truly converted to the central teaching of Jesus: love your enemies.

Likewise, St. Paul wrote: "They will be punished with everlasting destruction and shut out from the presence of the Lord and from the glory of his might" (2 Thessalonians 1:9). The contemporary mystic Richard Rohr, in collaboration with the Center for Action and Contemplation, presents an alternate and wise view:

> Jesus tells us to love our enemies (Matthew 5:44), but the punitive god sure doesn't. Jesus tells us to forgive "seventy times seven" times (Matthew 18:22), but this other god doesn't. Instead, this other god burns people *for all eternity.* Many of us were raised to believe this, but we usually had to repress this bad theology into our unconscious because it's literally *unthinkable.* Most humans are more loving and forgiving than such a god, but we can't be more loving than God. It's not possible. This "god" is not God![8]

A God who torments souls nonstop for all eternity is one who does not follow the Sermon on the Mount or even have the mature loving consciousness that motivated spiritually conscious humans such as Gandhi and Martin Luther King Jr. To believe in a God like that makes going beyond retaliation impossible. Likewise, believing there is a hell means believing that retaliatory punishment is acceptable, even required. We want to ask ourselves about holding that unkind belief in our hearts. It does not sit in us like a robin singing; it sits on us like a scorpion striking. Which do we choose to give hospitality to?

Mark Twain said that God made us in his own image and that we then returned the favor. The God who reflects the inflated vindictive ego is not the God of compassion and forgiveness but the god of punitive retribution. Is that the God we would want to be with for all eternity? If we hear ourselves saying, "But sinners, those other people, deserve hell!" our work is still waiting for us, and so is finding a God we can love. "Hell" is also a striking metaphor for a world hopelessly aflame with injustice, war, and hate. "Can I have and hold on to heart even in this?"

I was fortunate several years ago to attend a lecture in Santa Barbara given by the Tibetan Buddhist scholar Robert Thurman. He gave us a short exercise that helped me a lot: He asked us to close our eyes and "picture Hitler where we imagine him to be now." After a short time, he asked us to open our eyes and raise our hands if we pictured Hitler in hell. Of the three hundred or so people, almost every hand went up including mine. Then he asked us to close our eyes again and picture Hitler as a Buddhist monk sitting in the lotus position while a stern but gentle Zen master said to him over and over: "Remember what you did and ask forgiveness." Next Dr. Thurman asked us to imagine that this will go on for as long as it takes for him to see the light and then someday come back to earth as a most compassionate buddha intent on helping humans as much as he hurt them before. He then requested that we open our eyes and asked us which kind of energy we wanted to carry around in our heart, the first or the second— the hopeless, mean-spirited hell fire or the redeeming kindheartedness. Since a hell of punishment is only a metaphor, aren't we better off carrying around a love cameo in our hearts rather than a grotesque scene from Dante's *Inferno*?

JUDGMENT AND KARMA

In traditional Christian belief there awaits all of us the Last Judgment by which good people will go to heaven and non-contrite sinners will go to hell. This ego-satisfying belief assures us that God will finally join in the ego's heartless plans for revenge on quite a grand scale.

Both the Hebrew Bible and the New Testament present the tit-for-tat view:

"Who sows injustice will reap calamity" (Proverbs 22:8).
"As you sow so shall you reap" (Galatians 6:7).

Both Bible quotations have the cadence of retaliation: they will get theirs. Yet it is a given of life that the opposite can happen. We can sow injustice and have prosperity. We can sow goodness and reap calamity. We can more readily aver that "reap what we sow" works *internally*: "When I do good, I like myself more. Because of what I have sown I reap a good feeling in myself, a feeling of joy and a boost in self-esteem." Thus, the quotations are right on the interior level. But if what happens internally is fear of retaliation by God or fate, we are still not spiritually awake to the power of love.

In Eastern spiritual traditions, karma refers to the consequences of our intentions and actions. *Karma* is a Sanskrit word meaning "action" or "what is done." What happens to us is not based on a judgment by a divinity but a natural sequence of cause and effect. Ultimately karma is about what kind and how many rebirths a person may be subject to. When karma refers to punishment for our misdeeds, it becomes a form of retaliation. It is also another example of how we expect some force to enact vengeance for us on those who have harmed us. Now we are relying not on God but on fate to join us in revenge: "What goes around comes around. No matter how I may fail in retaliating there will be some other power to step in and accomplish it for me." In other words, revenge has to happen for me to be satisfied. But it proves to be only wishful thinking after all. The givens of life show again and again that is not the way the world works, the world in which the rains fall on the just and unjust alike, and the ocean waves buoy up the cruise and bomber ships with equal gusto.

A SPIRITUAL KOAN

Theodicy, the vindication of divine goodness in view of the existence of evil, attempts to deal with the question of how an all-good God could permit evil. If God is just, why do bad things sometimes happen to good people while good luck sometimes comes to bad people? Implicit in this question is the wishful thinking or belief that the good should be rewarded and the evil should be punished. Some act of divine justice should make sure that retribution will befall evildoers. The act of God can be a personal or a natural disaster affecting a whole group of offenders. Justice, in this context, is equated with retaliation against those who do wrong and reward for those who do good. That perspective ultimately panders to the vengeful ego that insists on vengeance. In the Bible Job wonders why he is being punished by God when he has lived such an upright life. Job saw personal suffering as indicative of divine punishment. That does not hold up as a valid conclusion given the frequency of the opposite occurring in human experience. Job believes that he deserves rewards for his virtue. That is not logical either, given the fact that life is not always a fair quid pro quo. In mature spiritual consciousness we have come to understand that *suffering is not a punishment and happiness is not a reward*. They are simply facts of human life. They are happenings, not results. The valid given of life is that things happen without respect to the goodness or badness of the people on whom they befall.

As we have seen, inherent in the human psyche is an expectation of punishment if we do wrong: suffering or hardship is somehow our fault. It also seems that in our collectively inherited belief system is the principle that reality/God/fate is vengeful. Our ego, the fierce opponent of powerlessness, needs to be in control by locating the reasons for a random adversity. Personal guilt is a facile answer: now we can declare that we are not victims while also admitting that we are offenders. None of this refers to instances in which we did indeed cause ourselves suffering—for example, not using a seat belt and having a car accident. Our topic is random disasters, illnesses, or accidents. We want an explanation, so we might conclude that it was the hand of fate.

Personal guilt is also an adaptive way we alert ourselves to atone and act more skillfully. Guilt followed by repentance can help us find closure—and get back in the driver's seat, this time on the road to wholeness.

Theodicy as a koan asks a question for which a logical answer is expected. But the answer to the question proposed in theodicy defies solution. Its answer is simply an unconditional yes to the way things are. With that liberating yes comes a letting go of all the whys. The magnificent result is a call to a spiritual practice. In Buddhism the answer to "Why is there evil?" is "I do all the good I can today." Thus, the answer is simply practice. We practice loving-kindness and all our quarrels with life's untidy conundrums fade away. "Why?" turns into "Yes!" and a whole new take on life unlocks in us when love is all that matters. We then find practices of integrity and loving-kindness that turn our original questions into commitments to make the world a better place, a place where there are no grounds for revenge. Could there be a more wonderful calling?

SIX

Forgiveness and Forgivingness

ONE WAY WE KNOW we love someone is that we can't stay mad at them for long and can't help but forgive them. Forgiveness can be described as a state of mind, or rather heart, that is free of blame, ill will, resentment, and retaliation toward an offender. Forgiveness is an innate interior setting in all of us that, when opened, will affect our response to an offense. We see in this that forgiveness is too complex to be reduced to stimulus-response. It can't be simply "You offended me. I forgive you. Now it's over." It will take grief to pave the way to forgiveness. We first let ourselves experience the sadness and anger components of grief. Here is an example of a healthy response to an offense: We are angry at the injustice done to us or to those we care about. We feel that anger but we hold the offense as a saddening fact, not as a trigger into retaliation. Nor do we blame, hold a grudge, feel ill will, or hold resentment toward the offender. Thus forgiveness is not a waiving of anger or an avoidance of feeling. That would mean denying an injury. We express our pain surrounding a betrayal or grievance and engage in a dialogue with the provoking party if we see an openness to that option. But instead of payback, we forgive back.

Forgiveness is free of vengeance because we are not engaging in the negative habit of answering hurt with hurt. We are doing what is altogether innovative rather than repetitive. We are not fettered by any need to mimic what was done to us nor by any need to repeat a trespass against our trespasser, which are the favorite customs of retaliation. Now we see how forgiveness can be a basis of hope in humanity, because we have it in us to begin again after being hurt. In the face of injustice, we can resist and be lovingly nonviolent. Hannah Arendt, in *The Human Condition*, wrote: "Forgiving . . . is the only reaction which does not merely re-act but acts anew and unexpectedly."[1]

FORGIVENESS VERSUS PARDON

Forgiveness is sometimes confused with pardon. We gain a depth understanding of forgiveness when we see how it differs from mere pardon. Let's look at the distinctions: To forgive is to dispatch an offense or debt, to absolve, to give up all claim on, to hold no resentment or grudge against. To pardon is to spare people from the consequences and penalties that attach to an offense, to acquit them from punishment.

Neither pardoning nor forgiving include condoning an offender's behavior. Forgiveness does not exculpate transgressors, but it does hold their guilt in a new container of compassion and non-retaliation. Pardon, too, does not condone a wrong, but it does excuse it from punishment.

As we saw at the beginning of this chapter, forgiveness is letting go of these four reactions: resentment, ill will, blame, and retaliation. Pardon lets go of retaliation but not necessarily of ill will, blame, or resentment. Both forgiveness and pardon are selective; they can be directed to this person and not to that one. Pardon lets someone off the hook this time but keeps the offense on the offender's permanent record. It can sound like this when it is conditioned by a warning that there can be no next time: "I will let it go this time." Or it might be "I'll let it go this time, but don't let me see your face around here again!" Forgiveness clears the slate entirely, without conditions.

The narcissistic ego has a major disability. It can't be unconditional in love or in any virtue. It has to be sure it comes out on top and is first at all times. The concerns of the inflated ego take precedence over the needs and feelings of others. This is why pardon is as far as an inflated ego can go. But a healthy ego can go the next step and forgive.

We can choose to pardon but we can't simply, by an act of will, make ourselves forgive. Forgiveness simply happens. It is an inner shift that occurs by the power of a grace, the gift dimension of life that can open us to an unconditional love and universal compassion. Anyone can, however, sincerely choose to act in nonretaliatory ways. We can practice acting with compassion—that is, we can act as if we had fully embraced nonretaliation. A new letting go then happens in us, and this is another example of grace kicking in. We suddenly notice we are no longer holding on to blame, ill will, resentment, or the desire to retaliate. In other words, forgiveness has happened in us as a graced response to someone's transgression.

Forgiveness and pardon do not have to be either/or. We may at any time find ourselves somewhere between the two. Pardon can be a path to forgiveness rather than a poor relation to it.

Shakespeare, in *The Tempest*, act 5, scene 1, clearly shows us the difference between forgiveness and pardon:

Though with their high wrongs I am struck to the quick,
Yet with my nobler reason [against] my fury
Do I take part: the rarer action is
In virtue than in vengeance

This is forgiveness since it is from the heart and unconditional—that is, not based on whether the offenders are sorry and repentant. The next lines show a conditional response to an offense:

> . . . they being penitent,
> The sole drift of my purpose doth extend
> not a frown further.[2]

This is pardon because it is based on *seeing* compunction and repentance in the offenders. Here is another example of perceiving a feeling of moral scruple in the offender: The person who hurt our feelings blushes in shame. We notice that we then automatically become more apt to reconciling. Actually, one of the reasons people blush is precisely to show compunction so as to offset the possibility of a retaliatory injury from the person they offended. So blushing is an adaptive measure by wrongdoers to ensure their safety and survival in a vengeful world.

Likewise, an offender offering an apology can revoke, or at least reduce, our rage. Such contrition in the other person can activate our innate capacity to let go, usually instantly, of any need to retaliate. Another example is one we may have noticed on the road: A driver cuts us off in traffic or acts discourteously to us. But he turns toward us with eye contact and a gesture that means "Sorry for that! My fault! I didn't mean it!" Our will to retaliate, our triggering into road rage, are both instantly quelled. The plan to exact vengeance has been eradicated by the contrition of the transgressor. And the offense is soon forgotten. Likewise, if the villain repents in a movie, or especially if he sacrifices himself for the hero, our wish for vengeance on him is instantly dispelled.

Finally, the word *remorse* is sometimes confused with repentance. Remorse is sorrow about what we have done, but not with contrition or commitment to a change, which are essential elements of repentance. We might feel remorse when we are called out for an offense we committed, but our sorrow is about getting caught! Likewise, remorse ends with itself, whereas repentance is a first step to new behavior. For example, we feel buyer's remorse because we paid too much for something. It ends there. When, on the other hand, we repent that we hurt someone's feelings, we show sorrow and promise to be more sensitive in the future. Judas felt remorseful and ended his life. Peter was repentant and began a whole new life of devotedness to his spiritual path.

PRACTICE

Five Steps to At-one-ment

We show atonement and repentance following steps like these:

1. We give a full account of what we did, including wrongful actions the other person may not know about: "Here is the whole truth about what I did."
2. We show and say that we are contrite—that is, genuinely sorry and regretful that we caused harm: "I am really sorry for what I did."
3. We apologize by admitting that we did something that was unfair or unloving and that we were wrong in doing it. An apology is real when we take responsibility for our behavior rather than using excuses. "Please accept my sincere apology."
4. We make amends and make reparations for our offenses in accord with the other person's openness to it. This includes recompense and restitution whenever possible. "I offer to make up for what I did."
5. We commit ourselves not to repeat the offense. This is what contributes to the rebuilding of trust in us by the offended person. "I am committing myself to not do this again."

When we have offended others we might also find comfort in these words in Sophocles' play *Antigone* that join repentance practice with love: "Think: all men make mistakes, but a good man yields when he knows his course is wrong, and repairs the evil. The only crime is pride."[3] (*Pride* refers to the ego refusal to admit being wrong or to forgive the wrongs of others.)

Sophocles shows how our penitence is a sweet spur to being loved by others. Unfortunately, there are people who don't want that loving inclusion. Let's look at a possible sequence: people sometimes harm others. Conscience admonishes them, and they then turn to healthy or primitive options: One person repents and makes changes for the better. Another person refuses forgiveness and insists on self-punishment—Oedipus blinding himself for his wrongs is an example.

For society to evolve in beneficial ways, it has to offer a way of dealing with misdeeds, of having the miscreant become a useful member of society again. Throughout the ages rituals have evolved to meet that need. We see them coming to us from society, religion, and spiritual traditions. Examples are prophets advising repentance, Twelve Step recovery programs with a focus on amends, the Truth and Reconciliation Commission project, and prison reform. All offer resources for guilty people to clear their conscience, make restitution, and rejoin society.

Most people take advantage of the humane options of forgiveness and absolution. Yet, sadly, some people can't allow that closure. They insist that their crimes are too gigantic and require self-punishment in the form of lifelong regret. This is denying the possibility of recovery, rejecting the grace of forgiveness—acts that makes us wonder if an ego is at the helm. Refusing to find self-forgiveness is a sad form of self-retaliation. We can feel compassion for people in that predicament and check in with ourselves to see if we are there too in any way.

FREEDOM FROM GUILT

Buddhist teacher Dogen Zenji wrote: "With repentance you will certainly receive invisible help from buddha ancestors. Repent to the buddhas with mind and body. The power of repentance melts the roots of unwholesomeness."[4] If we have hurt someone's feelings and made sincere amends, we are no longer guilty. There may also be times when we did not intend harm but someone felt harmed nonetheless. In that instance, we do not experience guilt but we are sorry that the other feels hurt. We did not mean to cause harm but our actions or words somehow triggered hurt feelings in the other person. We listen without being defensive and engage in a conversation to explore what really happened for each of us. We distinguish our good intention from its negative impact but do not let ourselves off the hook because our intention was positive. We may learn to be more sensitive toward that person in the future. It is a given of life that knowing others, or ourselves, will take an unending discussion—just what finding any truth requires.

If someone believes she has been targeted by us and does not speak up and say so until a while later, we might say to ourselves: "It's on her now for not speaking up sooner. I don't have to apologize now. After all, she held on to resenting me far too long." That is the voice of the judgmental, entitled ego showing its inability to be magnanimous. In unconditional love neither the other's timing nor his lack of timely assertiveness matters. Who did, or did not do what, or why, or when does not weigh in. Love counts but does not keep count.

Sometimes retaliation is disguised as if it were humorous. In a group there is someone who once offended us. We come at him with sarcasm or a put-down that has a mean edge to it. In this instance, we might catch ourselves and unabashedly call ourselves out: "Hey, I just realized that wasn't funny and I apologize." We are thereby humbly admitting our blunder and showing we are sorry for it. Most people will respect us for being like that. But our motive in spiritual practice is never to gain applause. It is to act in accord with our commitment to work on ourselves. Part of that work is self-correction and acceptance of accountability. Our openness takes us to a self-forgiving port in all our shipwrecks.

When an offense is collective, perpetrated by a whole group against another group, atonement will likewise be collective. Our nation apologizing and making amends for our genocidal actions against Native Americans, with the world watching, would be an example.

Simply accepting punishment while not experiencing a change of heart or contrition about our transgressions does not constitute true atonement. Punishment can facilitate atonement, but sometimes it does not. We are not atoning when we go kicking and screaming to our punishment while refusing to acknowledge our misdeeds. On the other hand, punishment from the state for the robbery we have committed is a form of penal redress that we may not welcome but are willing to undergo, believing we owe for our crimes.

FORGIVING AND FORGETTING

We can forget an offense rather than keep it alive as resentment, or we can refuse to forget an offense and keep retaliating. Forgetting, in the sense of holding something against someone, is a player in both instances. What is the relationship between forgiving and forgetting? The theologian Paul Tillich wrote: "I speak of the last willingness to accept him who has hurt us. Such forgiveness is the highest form of forgetting, although it is not forgetfulness . . . Forgetting in spite of remembering is forgiveness."[5]

A narrative memory can't be consciously erased but we can be free of its sting by no longer holding an offense against someone.

In forgiveness it is the tie to the past memory that is severed once and for all. That is how forgiving and forgetting happens. Forgiveness is thus quite radical because it undermines the central premise of revenge: keep the grudge alive. The forgetting does not mean we won't remember a wrong, only that it soon becomes simply information rather than a trigger into resentment and revenge. We remember what happened as a story, a news item without any negative editorializing of it on our part.

Forgiveness as forgetting can be practiced symbolically too, as a touching moment in the past illustrates. The Civil War ended on April 9, 1865. When the news reached Washington, DC, a large crowd gathered at the White House. President Lincoln came out and joyfully asked the band to play "Dixie." He reclaimed the southern anthem for all to partake in. His choice of that song also symbolized forgetting division and affirming unity among the states. How apt that forgiveness happens as an ending of war.

PRACTICE

Five Steps to Forgiving Others

We may not be successful at forgiving at times. What matters, always, is the purity of our intention, not success in every practice. We can always make an aspiration: "May I open my heart more and more to the gift of showing forgiveness."

How do we hold the intention and make the choices that help us move us toward forgiving our trespassers? Here is an updated practice from my book *The Five Longings: What We've Always Wanted and Already Have* (Shambhala, 2017) that has worked well for me and others. We keep in mind that forgiveness is practice, not passivity. To forgive is not to become a doormat. It is to widen the door into effective loving. Every human will err and every loving person can forgive. The following list of practices will also serve as a summary of what we have explored so far in this book:

1. Whenever you are offended or hurt, let yourself first grieve the pain—that is, feel your sadness, anger, and fear. The refusal to forgive is first of all a refusal to grieve, the experience that best leads to letting go of ill will, blame, resentment, and retaliation. Grieving and letting go of these four comprises forgiveness. Forgiveness is not a technique but a spiritual commitment. Once we notice we can forgive more and more, two wonderful shifts occur: we no longer feel like victims and we realize that no wrong is unforgivable. Notice if such shifts are happening in you.

2. Abstain from acting on hate, resentment, and retaliation. We may not be able to let go of these as thoughts but we can maintain control over whether we will act them out. The Dalai Lama says that now he no longer even thinks of revenge in response to harm done to him. That is a lot to expect of ourselves, but eventually, with ongoing practice, it may happen in us too. For now, *our spiritual practice of going beyond retaliation is complete just by not acting it out or by having the best intention not to show it, though occasionally our resolve may weaken.* When we do notice we have unconsciously retaliated, we apologize and become more vigilant thereafter.

3. Imagine that you are holding the memory of the hurt in your generous heart, not in your affronted ego. This is holding the intention to forgive the people who have offended you. It is a shift from exclusion to inclusion. We hold those who have hurt us as in a locket close to our heart, not as locked out. We can also place all that others do and all that we do in the heart of our higher power. There is always room in the sacred heart of our higher self, and never enough room in the heartless ego.

4. Say yes to the given of life that people are sometimes mean and unfair or may disappoint, hurt, or betray you. This is letting go of resistance to the reality of the negative side of humans, and we can now do so with deep compassion:

- We were taught to harm those who hate us. We have it in us to do good those who hate us.
- We were taught to curse those who curse us. We have it in us to bless and wish the best for those who curse us.
- We were taught to get back at those who mistreat us. We were taught that truly bad people forfeit any right to loving-kindness. We have it in us to pray or wish for enlightenment for those who mistreat us. This does not mean we put up with abuse. We still defend ourselves, but nonviolently and non-vindictively.
- We were taught to look out for number one. We have it in us to love without ranking. We commit ourselves to a radical mutuality. We are ready to transmute our ego-centeredness into heart-centeredness no matter what we were taught. The ever-illuminating heart of the universe has become our teacher, inviting us to share its radiant Dharma with others.

5. Engage daily in the Buddhist practice of loving-kindness using these aspirations that reflect the four qualities of an enlightened person:

- May I and all beings open to loving-kindness.
- May I and all beings show compassion.
- May I and all beings let go of envy, be happy about one another's successes, and be there for one another in times of loss or defeat.
- May I and all beings have equanimity in all that happens to us.

In Buddhism the above four qualities of our enlightened nature are loving-kindness, compassion, joy at others' success, and equanimity. Implicit in living out our Buddha nature is a commitment to nonretaliation, since loving-kindness, compassion, and joy at others' success are the opposites of retaliation. And equanimity is freedom from being triggered into retaliating. As long as we are still retaliating, we are not truly committed to acting in accord with our Buddha nature. The fact that the four qualities are called "immeasurable" helps us understand what unconditionality, universality, unreservedness, and unending are about. The qualities are immeasurable in all four senses: they are unconditional in how they are shown, universal in how far they extend, unreserved in how generously they are given, and unending in how long they are to last.

***

THE VIRTUE OF FORGIVINGNESS

There is a third alternative to pardon and forgiveness: forgivingness. Martin Luther King Jr., in *Strength to Love*, described it perfectly: "Forgiveness is not an occasional act; it is a permanent attitude."[6] I refer to that permanent, unconditional state of the heart by the word "forgivingness." In forgivingness there is no longer any dualism, no offender or forgiver. We forgive because we are forgiveness. We live forgivingly all the time. Pardon eliminates consequences; forgiveness clears all accounts. Forgivingness keeps no ledger at all.

This same distinction applies to love. For the virtue of loving-kindness toward others to be real, it can't be based on whether we see lovability in the other. We love because we love, not because of how appealing someone is. We know our love for others is real when their moments of unlovability no longer matter or trigger us.

Forgivingness is a virtue—that is, a habit of goodwill that is likewise a spiritual commitment. Forgivingness, like any virtue, originates in a transformation that has happened to us, and we are now continually showing its effects in our attitudes and actions. It becomes our go-to in the face of an offense. The Roman philosopher Seneca noticed this transition in himself: "He was always the same and consistent with himself in every act; not 'good' by design, but so thoroughly habituated that he not only could act rightly but could not act other than rightly. We understood that in him virtue was complete."[7] In other words, virtue is a quality of being, it is who we are or have become.

As with all virtues, we can also simply act in a virtuous way though we may not have the full virtue—that is, we have not yet built the habit. For example, a person who does not have the virtue of patience can, in special circumstances, be patient. A dad is ordinarily impatient. But when his daughter is in the emergency room he waits patiently for the doctor's report. With practice he can be patient all the time. Likewise, we can practice forgiving more and more, and that can turn into the virtue of forgivingness. Practice with effort and shifts by grace are commonplace in spiritual practice.

To summarize, we can say that in developed spiritual consciousness, forgivingness means that we are only love and forgiveness no matter the circumstance or person or whether, when, or why. Our response to offenses is never retaliation and always forgiveness. Unconditional love and unconditional forgiveness, forgivingness, thus signal how a major change has happened in how we relate, which is a release from the ego with all its gold medals for successful retributions, all its glee about achieving tit-for-tat. But in the great awakening there is no offense, nor anything left to forgive.

When we live by the virtue of forgivingness we need no reason or motive for forgiving other than the fact of our common humanity. We may practice forgiveness when we feel our hearts tugged by offenders' suffering, when we understand the motives behind their offenses, or when we receive their apology. But in forgivingness all those considerations and requirements have become irrelevant and all that matters is our indissoluble connection as humans. There is no slate to clear, no apology to wait for, no amends to be demanded, no motive for resentment, or no reason for revenge.

SELF-RETALIATION AND SELF-FORGIVENESS

It has been said that having a desire for vengeance is like drinking poison and waiting for the other person to die. Every choice for payback is also a choice to coarsen our hearts. Since our hearts are inside us, they stay hardened not only toward others but toward ourselves. Retaliation is a form of suffering for both perpetrator and victim. An offender does something that leads to suffering in the victim. Then the victim reciprocates, and so the cycle of pain continues. Suffering becomes the cause and result of retaliation.

Retaliation is turning on others. Self-retaliation is turning on ourselves, self-sabotage. Let's look at a prime source of self-retaliation: believing in and obeying the decrees of the inner critic. This is the scolding voice resident within us that may resemble put-downs or criticisms from childhood. This is the inner bully who pummels us, especially when we are most vulnerable. When we take that critical voice seriously, we become tyrants over ourselves. We then engage in self-harm or self-abnegation, we are turning on ourselves. To try to get rid of parts of ourselves that the inner critic or other people have deemed unworthy is to turn their aggression on ourselves. Self-acceptance is the opposite of such self-punishment.

The inner critic may want us to believe that we are isolated prey with nothing going for us. We mistakenly imagine we are trapped in our suffering. Hope flourishes when we realize we have resources. Our main inner resource is our own Buddha nature: a presence that is intimately with us and never lets us go, no matter how dark the day or how dark our deeds. *Anxiety, fundamentally, is doubting that presence.* Buddha nature may not tell us its name, but it names itself in our turning toward goodness because it is goodness, or rather, it is we who are goodness. Our true identity is wider than the inner critic has noticed. It is up to us to welcome our inner critic into the vastness of our Buddha nature, the radical wonderfulness of being human.

We also have abundant resources all around us, such as assisting forces in the form of supportive people. An assisting force is a healing third entity emerging from the dualism of predator (the inner critic) and victim—both of which are ultimately only ourselves. Our illusory world of wolves and lambs is beautifully balanced by the presence of assisting forces, those helpful sheepdogs!

As an aside, I notice a special power in these analogies from nature. They never fail to unearth a vein of hope in any of our human perplexities. Awareness of, wonder at, and trust in nature is a sanctuary of encouragement when the inner critic tells us we have nothing going for us. Nature's way is always the antidote to despair since it includes the certainty of renewal, restoration, and revitalization, the causes of optimism. We see that floods encourage new growth, withering spirals into blooming, and endings cycle into openings. The shy light of sunrise opens into the light of day. Human life can be an adventurous journey through a jungle of lush surprises and tiger-bright dangers that serve to strengthen us at every turn. Our fidelity to that path of hope is exponentially powerful as we face the inner critic, that would-be captain of despair.

Retaliation is aggression-provoked aggression. The inner critic is aggressive toward us and we are aggressive in return, but toward ourselves. When a bully hits us, we might take it or run away.

When the inner-critic bully hits us we take it, hit ourselves, and stay put for more. As the judgmental inner critic takes charge more and more, we might retaliate against ourselves in ways like these:

- We listen to our inner critic and accept its put-downs; we put ourselves down.
- We belittle ourselves.
- We believe we have nothing going for us.
- We see ourselves as inadequate.
- We let people shame, intimidate, manipulate, or bully us because we believe we deserve that.
- We don't stand up for ourselves.
- We engage in health-harming addictions.

These are all forms of self-loathing, which is another name for self-harm, and harming is of course what revenge is about. Our concern in this book is not only about how we have to tend to our relationships with others. It applies also to how we can tend our own fragile hearts with compassion for the ways we take revenge on ourselves.

PRACTICE

Affirming Self-Forgiveness

An alternative to self-retaliation is self-forgiveness. When we forgive ourselves for past mistakes and misdeeds, we let go of regret—that is, of self-blame, which is the opposite of self-forgiveness. We hold our regrets in the spiritual container of *saying yes to the inevitable limitations that are part of every human life*. This *yes* is the positive reframing of regrets. We can relate to our limitation rather than let it decimate our self-esteem. God within, or Buddha nature, means that the brokenness is itself God and enlightenment. It is precisely our resistance to our broken selves that blocks our access to the divine within us. When we feel no shame in being limited, we have embraced the virtue of humility. We are then no longer able to feel humiliated. We hear the inner critic or anyone's judgment of us as information, as a teaching that leads to a spiritual practice. Then we calmly notice that we are no longer bullied, no longer shamed, no longer afraid of anyone, not even the bullying critic inside us.

Here are affirmations that can lead to self-forgiveness and self-compassion:

- More and more I am all-accommodating toward my deficiencies and defects.
- I let go of my grievances against myself.
- I let go of being downtrodden by regrets.
- I make allowances for my limitations and errors.
- I turn my limits into daring initiatives.
- I see how much of what my parents, or other influencers, wanted me to do or to think was right was based on their own beliefs and fears. I forgive them.
- I see my wounds as portals into self-compassion.
- Now I think of each inner put-down as a teaching.
- I rethink my beliefs about the givens of life and the people in my life; they are all now part of my daily *yes*.
- I show myself the five As that demonstrate authentic love: attention to my feelings, needs, and longings; affection toward my body by caring for my physical and mental health; appreciation of my struggles and my attempts to handle them; acceptance of myself just as I am; and allowing myself to live in accord with my own deepest needs, values, and wishes.
- Now I hold my inner critic in the container of the Dharma so that it is gradually converted to Buddhism and practices loving-kindness toward me.

We can grow in self-forgiveness by letting go of the four opponents of forgiveness: blame, ill will, resentment, retaliating:

- More and more I let go of blaming myself while still being accountable.
- I show goodwill to myself, no longer engaging in what harms me or hating myself for being me.
- I give up being angry at myself, especially about my mistakes.
- I let go of turning on myself and of wanting to shame or punish myself.

As we incorporate these affirmations into our daily lives, we feel ourselves moving toward full self-forgiveness and full loving-kindness toward ourselves, wounds, warts, faults, and all. We also feel more compassion for people in our own lives and on the world stage who are still so futilely engaged in self and other vengeance.

We take what our inner critic batters us with, such as shame, and we realize that others feel it sometimes too. We then combine self-compassion with compassion for others rather than flagellate ourselves for being less than everyone else. We may then hear ourselves affirm: "I have all that it takes to love myself right now no matter how messed up I am, and I hope everyone else does this for themselves too."

Our experience of self-compassion and self-forgiveness thus leads to compassion for others since it is a given of life that we are all broken in some way. We all offend; we all make mistakes; we all need forgiveness. All we human blunderers await compassion, love's salute to us when we stand at attention.

Finally, we can apply mindfulness to how we hear the inner critic. In mindfulness we let go of judgment, control, limiting definitions, personal interpretations, shame, fear, and craving. We simply accept the here-and-now version of ourselves just as we are with a fulsome welcome. When we do exactly that regarding our limitations, we are free of the chains clamped around our hearts by our inner critic. We are then allowed the freedom to love ourselves because our compassion for ourselves and everyone else has finally fully bloomed.

THE DIFFERENCE BETWEEN JUDGING AND ASSESSING

In all of the above practices we may find ways to reframe the judgments of the inner critic so that they become helpful feedback. In this way, the judgments that would have become self-retaliatory turn into opportunities to forgive ourselves and learn from ourselves as well.

There are also times when we are judgmental of others or they are judgmental toward us. In Buddhism there is a practice called "right [appropriate] speech." Being judgmental about other people's behavior or attitudes does not seem skillful or appropriate for those on the journey to enlightenment. Yet what is called "judgmental" may actually be constructive feedback. What's the difference? In the chart below, we distinguish being judgmental from healthy assessing and the giving of helpful feedback. This applies to how we see others, how they see us, and how we see ourselves.

BEING JUDGMENTAL	INTELLIGENTLY ASSESSING
Based on blaming and jumping to conclusions	Based on diligent discerning
Attacks the other	Opens a dialogue
Focuses on who did it and how that person messed up	Focuses on what happened and how we can mend it
Is censuring	Is commenting
Comes at the other, like it or not and irrespective of appropriate timing	Asks if the other is open to a conversation and respects the other's timing
May use put-downs, name-calling, and insults	Gives well-meant feedback
Shames the other: "You are bad or wrong."	Informs the other: "Here is something to examine."
States: "I am totally right on this."	Acknowledges: "I may be inaccurate."
Wants the other to squirm	Wants the other to feel cared about and seen
Feels unsafe and intrusive	Feels safe and respectful
Feels like it has intimidation in it	Feels like it comes from goodwill
Implies: "You are not as good as I am."	Makes no comparisons
Closes off communication	Welcomes dialogue
Is reductive: "You are only this."	Affirms: "I know there is a lot more to you."

Draws conclusions about someone's behavior without evidence	Inquires into the other's behavior to ask about motives and meanings
Is personal and may be biased by projections, hurt, or fear	Remains neutral and relational, always attempting to be objective
Is meant to benefit one's ego	Is meant to share with the other person
Can have a retaliatory motive or be a preamble to retaliation	Has no connection to payback or lingering resentment
May turn into bad-mouthing and gossip	Remains confidential
Comes from an inside to an outside, a subject to an object: an I-It transaction	Comes from inside to inside, subject to subject: an I-Thou relationship
Labels someone's behavior, which can lead to objectifying and distancing	Empathizes with someone's suffering or inadequacy, which can lead to compassion, forgiveness, and a closer bond
May show no caring about hurting others' feelings	Comes from caring about and getting the best to happen for all concerned
Is meant to criticize in a dismissive way	Is taken seriously and meant to lead to repair
This is aggressive and divisive speech.	This is a mindful practice, a form of loving-kindness, and right speech.

Let's look at a specific example of the difference. To call yourself or someone else stingy is judgmental. When you look more closely you may see anxiety about giving, donating, or spending based on a long-standing fear of scarcity. That is an assessment. Judgment shames and holds hostility. Assessment recognizes suffering and feels compassion. The former forecloses on closeness. The latter fosters it. In this example we see that when we judge, there is more going on than just passing a verdict. That "more" is the possibility of losing closeness and compassion. A label does not lead to knowledge or love. We only truly know or love someone when we see that person with unconditional compassion. What is our life together about if not that?

SEVEN

Love and Revenge in
Intimate Relationships

HOW MANY PEOPLE in relationship would ever ask themselves: "Is there anything I am doing to my partner that is actually about payback? If yes, how can I say I love my partner if I keep doing this?" Most of us don't notice how vengeful attitudes and actions creep into our relationships.

Working with a couple in therapy one day I noticed that Matt had been deliberately triggering his wife Jane Ann into frustration and anger that week by doing things to upset her. Matt had already listed the ways she had annoyed him in recent months. I suddenly recognized what Matt had been up to that week; he was retaliating. I asked him directly if his actions were his way of getting back at Jane Ann. Matt stared at me in a way that showed I had hit the nail on the head. He, like me, had put a name on his deliberately annoying behavior. He then sheepishly replied: "Yes, I guess I am doing things to get back at her." Jane Ann admitted she was doing the same at times. I then realized that retaliation was a back-and-forth pattern by which these partners could remain angry at each other, a way of ensuring distance while still continuing the relationship. Retaliating can save people from the closeness they fear but may never name.

I can say that more than half of the one thousand partners and couples I have seen in therapy over the years engaged in subtle or open forms of retribution against each other. Most never put the name *retaliation* to their behavior. This is true of retaliation in general. We just don't name what we are doing. And not to name is not to know oneself. Is that also what we are up to in all this drama?

Love can flourish between people only when we notice and give up retaliation. In this chapter we will explore that option in the context of intimate relationships. We always keep in mind that retaliation is a form of suffering, so compassion will be important to our full understanding.

We can ask the question "How can two apparent opposites such as love and revenge coinhabit a love relationship?" We may first wonder if there is something about love that *has* to lead to suffering. Does loving someone automatically and eventually bring out the worst in us? Are we doomed to hurt the one we love? Why does embracing inevitably lead to scraping? Why does "You are in my heart" someday become "You get on my nerves"? What oxymoronic couplings, what strange bedfellows indeed, are love and revenge.

Many relationships that seem to be based entirely on love, including family relationships, have a love-hate element in them. We love someone but also hold some enmity toward them. Usually this double feeling goes unnoticed, sometimes by both people, even for a lifetime. We uncover our love-hate when we see ourselves pick a fight or act aggressively, spitefully, or in vindictive ways. We might even involuntarily feel schadenfreude when the other person is having a hard time. It takes ruthless self-inquiry for us humans to know all that is really going on in us when love is in the air. Nonetheless, we can always act in loving ways no matter what may be lurking inside us. Love-hate in some of our relationships is normal, but dangerous when acted on.

Our topic is not at all new. St. Augustine, in his fourth-century *Confessions*, noticed the same disturbing progression in his relationships: "I sought an object for my love; I was in love with love, and I hated safety and a path free of snares. . . . I rushed headlong into love, by which I was longing to be captured. . . . My love was returned and in secret I attained the joy that enchains. I was glad to be in bondage, tied with troublesome chains, with the result that I was flogged with the red-hot iron rods of jealousy, suspicion, fear, anger, and contention."[1] He noticed that sparks automatically fly as a relationship moves from lovey-dovey to push-pull. Is the inevitability of suffering the chilling fate of every love? Writing this now gives me a chill. I am asking a question I don't like asking. My own experience and that of so many clients I have seen as a psychotherapist makes me affirm that our negative shadow side emerges front and center when we are in an intimate relationship.

What we have been referring to as the negative shadow side is Carl Jung's phrase to describe unnoticed, undesirable traits in ourselves that we have disavowed all our lives. We know these traits are socially taboo, politically incorrect, and dangerous to lovability, sometimes even to our survival. So over the years we lock them away, especially from ourselves. We can think of our negative hidden self as a collection of ego-driven, divisive, mean-spirited, vindictive impulses that we might never imagine or believe were in us. Yet they peep out, pop out, when love is in the air for a while. They do not make their entrance early on in the romance phase when we are sure we have met our ideal partner and everything is going swimmingly. They make their appearance only when the hard-nosed ego meets a partner's hard-nosed ego and conflicts begin to drown the good feelings we had been so sure would never end. Now we hear ourselves saying and see ourselves doing what we never imagined was in us. We may even find out we have a mean streak, which is so often the lightning strike of vengeance. Could it be that knowing ourselves all the way to the bottom is as important to our psychic development as maintaining a healthy bond? Is that a clue to why such a dreary sequence occurs in a relationship?

Some of us, instead of taking the opportunity to know ourselves by seeing how we relate to a partner, may deny we have a shadow side at all. Instead, blaming our partner becomes our go-to. We engage in self-justification: "She brings out the worst in me, so it's her fault. I am not really like this." If we are committed to working on ourselves, the beginning of the work is knowing ourselves—that is, seeing the entire version of who we are, all sides accounted for. To do this we will have to let go of self-justifying excuses and blaming our partner, a humbling task that a big-shot ego may not permit.

Retaliation follows with great celerity on the heels of blame. As we have seen, payback is not necessarily a mirror-imaging. Retaliation does not have to mean doing to him what he did to me: "He had an affair and I am not going to do the same. But I am going to remind him of his guilt by blaming, shaming, and rubbing his nose in it, over and over. I am paying him back by doing the many little irritating things that drive him up a wall." And *wall* is just the word that names what is going up in the relationship.

In any case, our choice to be mean or to retaliate, as well as how we do it and to whom, can't help but eventually reveal us to ourselves once we really examine what we are up to. We find out if we really love someone, for instance, when we forgo recrimination in favor of its opposite, forgiveness. We do not excuse, but neither do we condemn our offenders. Removing meanness and retaliation from our repertory of responses toward a partner certainly makes the case that we are committed to cultivating an intimate connection. A firm commitment to ever-recurring kindliness, forgiveness, magnanimity, and reconciliation are a proof of love if there ever was one—or rather if there ever is to be oneness.

WHEN WE HURT THE ONE WE LOVE

We may still be wondering why people do things at times that hurt those they love.[2] Here is a chain of feeling-laden events that can happen when there is conflict in a close relationship. Looking at this possible sequence may help us understand the enigma.

1. We find someone who fulfills our needs.
2. We then become dependent on that person for the ongoing fulfillment of our needs.
3. The part of our ego that wants to assert independence feels resentful. We can't stand needing someone so much; it makes our ego feel weak. "I am angry at you for having this much power over me. How dare you make me need you."
4. Now the door is open for us to engage in passive or active aggression and retaliation in big or little ways.
5. So we feel we have the right to hurt and retaliate against the one we love.

We might also be hurting the one we love for one or more of these three reasons: resentment, fear, transference.

Resentment: We feel an ongoing resentment, engage in constant accusing, and hold a grudge against our partner. We wait for our chance to retaliate the minute she gives us what we see as a solid reason.

Fear: We are feeling engulfed and smothered by our partner and we resort to a primitive form of pushing away, retaliation. If we feel intimidated but are too scared to speak up, we may engage in retaliation in the form of passive-aggressiveness. We find a way to hit back while not having to be found out. We are aggressive on the sly.

Transference: Our earlier life experiences from traumatic past relationships or from childhood induce us to see the original culprit's face on our partner. We now have our chance for payback against the original offenders by directing it to the new partner.

PRACTICE

From Hiding to Opening

Now let's take a look at a practice of repair:

1. To look at a relationship with total honesty we ask ourselves how it has love in it, how it has resentment, fear, and transference in it. Most intimate relationships have all four going on at one time or always. This is nothing to be ashamed of. Looking at it all honestly, without shaming ourselves or blaming our partner, is what can make a difference.

2. We look at our feelings and behaviors honestly and find out what we may be up to when we engage in passive-aggressive behaviors that are, in reality, retaliation.

3. We ask if our partner may be doing all of the above to us. Then we ask for a "state of union" discussion with our partner and we both take responsibility for our part in what is going on.

4. Either way, together we will, without blame or release from accountability, commit ourselves to addressing, processing, and resolving our issue. Our goals are to make love primary, not to have no more resentment, fear, or transference in the relationship. But now they will be easily spotted and then dealt with openly. That is the real change: from unnoticed, unadmitted, and passive to noticed, admitted, processed, and resolved. All this will happen faster after the first brave step one.

Commitment to this fourth part of the practice is a sure sign of a truly adult partnership. This is because the greatest fear in a relationship is not the fear of closeness. It is the fear of being an adult in relationship to another adult.

MINOR AND MAJOR TRUST ISSUES

Revenge is reactive or reciprocated aggression, the opposite of healthy relating and reciprocal affection. However minor, tit-for-tat responses between partners do not repeal a contract of love. Likewise, turning a knee-jerk reaction to a trigger into spite does not mean we do not love someone. Some triggered reactions are unskillful behaviors but lack an intention to do damage and certainly are not based on ill will. We take such minor offenses in stride—we don't let them cancel trust or lead to revenge. Thus they can coexist with love. Now let's look at these distinctions in detail.

When retaliation is meant to hurt the other person, a relationship of love has been temporarily disabled. When retaliation ends with a commitment not to engage in it again, love can be restored. Minor acts of retaliation punctuate love but do not put a strikethrough on it.

In a conscious, mature relationship we trust a partner when we see that he has given up ordinary retaliation and would never engage in hateful revenge. Once a partner is on the lookout for his inveterate habit of retaliation and catches himself before he engages in that behavior, trust can be restored. But it may take a while for a partner to let go of a long-standing habit. "I may retaliate out of habit, and when I do I will apologize, make amends, and redouble my vigilance so I don't fall into it the next time I find myself triggered by what you say or do." We can trust the person who sincerely said that.

Severe mean-spirited revenge is altogether different. Revenge, as we saw above, is always deliberate, not an involuntary reflex. It is motivated by hate, so it cannot coexist with love. It includes ill will with a conscious attempt to harm or injure someone. People who love each other don't want to be the cause of suffering. This is why revenge, opposed as it is to trustful love, is never appropriate in an intimate relationship.

Someone who vengefully cuts us off forever after one offense did not love us to begin with and only felt good being with us on condition that we toed the mark—that is, the fierce mark of Zorro-ego.

Ego includes attachment to our version of ourselves, so that mindset opposes new emergent properties of intimacy between partners. In an intimate relationship we *want* our version of who we think we are to be confronted and challenged. Intimate partners welcome such evolutionary moments. These are the appropriate contexts for change and growth in us and they make for progress in intimacy. When ego is at the helm, however, we might be vengeful against a partner who dares to question our grandiosity. Now intimacy has flown away on vulture wings.

A CARING COMMITTED CONNECTION

If we think of love as a caring committed connection, we can easily see that each of the three elements can evoke fear. The fears originate in beliefs like these:

- If we care we might become vulnerable—and lose our position of control.
- If we stay committed we might lose our freedom—and lose our position of control.
- If we maintain connection we might be engulfed by the other—and lose our position of control.

With the price so high it is understandable that we become skittish. Our fears lead us to act out in ways that preserve our ego rather than our relationship. And ego's stock in trade is retaliation.

Ongoing retaliation or revenge revokes all three of the components of love:

- Caring can't happen when we are intent on hurting the other.
- Commitment can't happen when we retaliate rather than reconcile.
- Connection can't happen because retaliation has put it asunder.

A willingness to be vulnerable is requisite to all three elements of love:

- In our caring, we open ourselves to being unappreciated for it or being taken advantage of because of it.
- By our full commitment we accept the given of life that we might be betrayed.
- In maintaining connection we accept the possibility that the other person might abandon us.

In all three instances we chance the outcome of broken trust by our partner. When we are in a relationship with both feet we take that chance—this is also called openness to the givens of life and relationships. That openness is only tenable when we have inner resources to help us deal with whatever happens. We will handle whatever happens with strength and without retaliation. We also need assisting forces in and around us to help us get through the suffering and grief that may come our way. It is not useful to be vulnerable in a relationship unless we can also engage in self-care. This includes exiting the relationship if things don't change for the better and the safer. Healthy vulnerability is a welcoming of the whole gamut of love with self-care. Without it we are victims, not lovers.

GAMERS

Another motivation for retaliation in a relationship is the playing of a game. In this section we look at a mutual game, but we keep in mind that sometimes it is only one partner gaming. A game in a relationship refers to doing one thing while having it look like another, and it is usually motived by distancing. For example, we keep hurting each other, but staying together makes it look like we love each other. I am reminded of the lyrics from the old song "I Surrender, Dear" by Gordon Clifford and Harry Barris: "Little mean things we were doing / must have been part of the game, / lending a spice to the wooing."[3] We are mean to one another. We then engage in back-and-forth payback. We do this to play the game of fending off trust and closeness while still staying together. We don't really want trust and closeness. By competing in our revenges we are certainly maintaining distance and distrust. At the same time, we are still bonded, so it looks like we really are close to each other. A game fools us, lulls into obliviousness, and makes a trick look like love. The lyrics give a reason for this love-defeating behavior: it lends a spice to the wooing. In other words, we greatly enjoy the adrenaline-rich drama we are staging.

Some partners occasionally retaliate against each other. But when partners get off on continual back-and-forth retaliations, they are addicted to a game that underlies and perpetuates stress, opposition, and drama. The sexual aspect of such a relationship will be especially satisfying because it furthers the delusion that we are indeed being intimate. Sex and revenge can keep a game in motion long beyond the wooing.

When the motivation for the game is fear of closeness, we notice that fear often serves to keep everything in place. Fear protects the status quo. We tell ourselves not to change anything because we fear dire consequences. In reality the only consequence may be letting the truth come out so we can work on having a better relationship. Then the game ends and intimacy begins. Is that intimacy what we actually fear?

JUST TAKE IT?

We keep reminding ourselves that our letting go of retaliation is not passivity but practice. The questions that can then arise in a relationship are "Does commitment to the spiritual practice of going beyond retaliation mean that I let someone take advantage of me? How do I stay committed to going beyond retaliation yet take care of myself?" Satguru Sivaya Subramuniyaswami offers a response to such questions: "Some might ask, 'Does nonretaliation mean that one should not protect himself, his family, his community?' We are talking about revenge, not self-defense. To oppose the actions of an intruder to one's home or community at the time of the intrusion is very different from tracking him down later and vandalizing his home in retaliation."[4] The swami acknowledges the appropriateness of self-defense and an unremitting opposition to evil. Nonretaliation does not have to mean we don't stand up and fight, only that we fight in nonretaliatory ways. Such resistance to offense and abuse can happen using the skillful means of harm-avoidant yet militant nonviolence.

Revenge is aggression, an extreme reaction. "Walk all over me" is passivity, another extreme. We seek the middle path where inner resources bloom: self-healing skills and the strength to handle hurt feelings or to call out others' hurtful behavior. These are components of a gentle but firm assertiveness, which is so crucial if there is to be a successful partnership.

We can't avoid being offended from time to time, but we can learn how to handle the offense with kindly skill rather than by trying to do in the offender. This is another way to see being offended as a teaching. We place the offense into the context of learning about ourselves, others, and our opportunities for nonviolent relating. We then move from teaching to practice: we commit ourselves not to do to others what was done to us. Now our own suffering has led us to compassion toward those who offended us. We realize the offense came from the suffering in them. We have compassion for that suffering and then are more likely to forgive than retaliate.

Our compassion can lead to spiritual aspirations: "May those who have offended me be free of suffering and learn not to turn their own hurt into hurting others." We also have compassion for our own suffering: "I feel compassion for how I have been hurt. May I learn not to turn my hurt into hurting others." This is how the inescapable suffering we all experience—the first noble truth in Buddhism—can pave a path to enlightenment.

TEN PRACTICES OF LOVE
IN INTIMATE RELATIONSHIPS

1. Pausing, Placing, and Holding

When we are offended by a partner we pause, place, and hold:

Pausing: We take a mindful pause when we are triggered. This means letting ourselves see what has happened just as it is, without blame, judgment, name-calling, planning revenge, trying to control or change anything, or giving way to fear. The provocation from the other person becomes a news event, not an editorial.

Placing: We see an offense as information, a spiritual teaching, and an invitation to place it into the container of loving-kindness: "Where in my heart do I find room for this?" This is not denying that others sometimes act in unloving ways, only that we see what is unloving in a compassionate, understanding, loving way.

Holding: We hold the experience and our partner in our Buddha nature. We do not hold anything against the other. We make room for the other in our heart and keep him there. The alternative is holding a grudge in our retaliating ego. This is holding healing space.

2. Loving More

In daily interactions, partners can look for ways to show their love in an unconditional way:

> If love can't be the same between us two,
> I'll be the one to show more love to you.[5]

My verses suggest what unconditional love entails: we do not insist on even-steven but rather show unconditional generosity no matter what our partner does. As a practice, partners can tell each other if the poem describes their commitment. Relationships work only on the basis of at least one generous spirit, not on fulfilling the ego's demand that everything be equal.

3. Telling Our Plan

Regarding what is to be considered legitimate in one's repertory of behavior, partners can boldly and honestly state their personal plan directly to each other: "If you cross me I intend to retaliate," or "No matter how you upset me I will not retaliate but only say 'Ouch!' and try to open a dialogue so we can work things out. I have committed myself to nonretaliation as a spiritual path. I like myself this way. I am trying hard to live by this standard whether or not you abide by it too."

4. Solving for Safety

In a relationship in which retaliation is ongoing we are aware we feel unsafe or traumatized. We can declare aloud to our partner that we want to feel safe with them and can't if retaliation is still happening. We can talk about our spiritual practice of letting go of retaliation. We speak not to convince, only to inform. We say that continued retaliation is not sustainable, that we want a change in how we relate. Nonetheless, ours is a definite commitment to non-retaliation: "It ends with me."

5. Asking for Amends

In a relationship in which there has already been harm or abuse we can ask our partner for an acknowledgment of it, amends, and a commitment not to repeat it.

6. Blowing the Whistle

We recognize indirect aggression in ourselves or our partner and call it out. We then look together at feelings, motives, and past experiences, especially in childhood and in former relationships that are still unresolved. To find out what our priorities are in the relationship, we ask ourselves: "Do I want to get back at my partner or get our relationship back on track?"

7. Including the Relationship

We keep each other in our ongoing loving-kindness practice. When we do that, we make the relationship itself a subject of our practice, extending loving-kindness to our partnership, even when it is on the rocks.

8. Letting Go When You Are Gone

When a relationship ends, especially in a difficult divorce, the need to get revenge may take top billing in our minds. Our practice is exactly the same as in forgiveness: to let go of resentment, ill will, blame, and any need to retaliate.

9. Getting Help

Take advantage of a skilled helper in working through a conflict. We invest time and money well as we turn to a coach, mediator, or therapist to address, process, and resolve our issues.

10. Committing to Healthy Relating

We commit to honoring the following guidelines in all our relationships. Our commitment is not based on whether our partner or other people do so too. These points pull together what we have been exploring together so far in this book. We may choose to practice these commitments, follow these standards, one by one for a day or more at a time:

- I appreciate the ways others love me, no matter how limited. I am letting go of expecting—or demanding—that they love me exactly as I want them to. I am letting go of wanting others to prove that they love me. At the same time, I can always ask for the kind of love I long for.
- I remain open to reconciling with others after conflict. At the same time, I am learning to release—with love and without blame—those who show themselves to be unwilling to relate to me respectfully.
- I accept, without judgment, the given of sudden unexplained absence, ghosting, or the silent treatment by others and will not use those styles myself.
- When a family member suddenly cuts off communication with me, I ask for dialogue so we can repair the rupture. If the family member refuses, I respect that choice while remaining available for communication to resume. On my part, I choose not to ostracize family members who have offended me. Nor do I join other family members in their boycott against another

family member. When I meet up with family rejection, I grieve the situation and stay open to reconciliation.

- I do not knowingly hurt or intend to offend others. I act kindly toward others not to impress them, win their approval, or obligate them but because I really am kind—or working on it. If others fail to thank me or to return my kindness, that does not have to stop me from behaving lovingly nonetheless. When I fail at this—or at any of these commitments—I can admit it, make amends, and resolve to act differently next time. Now I can say "Oops!" more easily and willingly when necessary.

- If people occasionally hurt me, I can say "Ouch" (in lowercase letters or in all caps). I can ask to open a dialogue. I may ask for amends, but I can drop the topic if they are not forthcoming. No matter what, I do not choose to get even, hold grudges, keep a record of wrongs, or hate anyone. "What goes around comes around" has become "May what goes around come around in a way that helps everyone learn and grow." I am thereby hoping for the transformation of others rather than for retribution against them. I am seeking repair, not revenge.

- I know what it feels like when other people don't forgive me and I don't want to have others feel that way because of me. With compassion, I notice that my capacity to forgive others— and myself—is expanding. My forgiveness of others is a letting go of resentment, blame, ill will, and the need for revenge. This transformation by grace feels like a true liberation from ego.

- I see that my forgiving others can't be based on whether they are truly contrite or abase themselves to show they are. I recognize any demand like that on my part is another play for ego-triumph and retaliation. I want my forgiveness to be unconditional. Though I appreciate honest contrition or an apology, neither is necessary. What matters most now is honoring my own calling to be magnanimously loving toward all beings without reserve or requirement and without keeping score of offenses, even if repeated.

- I do not let others abuse me. I want to interpret their harshness as coming from their own pain and as a sadly confused way of letting me know they need connection but don't know how to ask for it in healthy ways. I recognize this with concern and compassion, not with censure or scorn.

- I do not gloat over the sufferings or defeats of those who have hurt me or those whom I dislike. "It serves them right!" has changed to "May this serve to help them evolve."

- I practice ways to express my anger against unfairness directly and nonviolently rather than in abusive, bullying, threatening, blaming, out-of-control, vengeful, or passive ways.

- I notice that there are people who are excluded from the in-group. Rather than be comforted that I am still safely an insider, especially by joining in gossiping about them, I want to sense the pain in being an outsider. Then I can reach out and include everyone in my circle of love, compassion, and respect.

- In a group situation, when someone is shamed, humiliated, or harshly criticized, I do not want to be glad that the finger was not pointed at me. I want to support the victim of aggression by asking for a respectful tone in the dialogue. I know that standing up for the victim may turn the bully's fury on me, so I continually work on building up my courage.

- I look at other people and their choices with intelligent discernment but without judgment or censure. I still notice the shortcomings of others and myself, but now I am beginning to see them as facts to deal with rather than flaws to be criticized or to be ashamed of. Accepting others as they are has become more important than whether they are what I want them to be.

- I am less and less competitive or oppositional in relationships at home and work and find happiness in cooperation and community. I avoid situations in which my winning means that others lose in a humiliating way. Winning is not at all my purpose in intimate relationships. Win-lose is dualistic and I want intimacy—and that is always nondual.

• I never give up on believing that everyone has an innate goodness and that when I show loving-kindness, I contribute to bringing it out.

EIGHT

From Payback to Love Back

MARTIN LUTHER KING JR., in his sermon "Loving Your Enemies," wrote:

> Throw us in jail and we shall still love you. Bomb our homes and threaten our children, and we shall still love you. Send your hooded perpetrators of violence into our community at the midnight hour and beat us and leave us half dead, and we shall still love you. But be ye assured that we will wear you down by our capacity to suffer. One day we shall win freedom, but not only for ourselves. We shall so appeal to your heart and conscience that we shall win you in the process and our victory will be a double victory.[1]

This is what is meant by over-the-top spiritual consciousness and practice. We love back no matter how others treat us, no matter how justified payback may seem. This is the lofty practice of showing love even if we are ambushed in the hell world of hate.

THE OPPOSITES

Retaliation is the exact opposite of the Golden Rule, the rule of mutual respect, the rule on which the social contract and human rights is based:

The Golden Rule: "Do to others as you want others to do to you. Do as you want to be done by." This is a path to reconciliation and unitive consciousness.

The Leaden Ego's Rule: "Do to others as they do to you. Do as you have been done by." This is the path of retaliation that

- polarizes, alienates, disconnects, breaks trust, dehumanizes the other
- escalates rather than regulates conflict and may lead to further escalation from the other side
- reinforces ego arrogance, entitlement, and the illusory sense of being in control
- hardens our hearts and disfigures our souls by triggering meanness—and may get that to happen in those against whom we retaliate
- breaks us apart rather than keeps us a part of the human community

Retaliation is also the exact opposite of the declaration made in the Lord's Prayer: "We forgive those who trespass against us." This is a pledge that we will let go of retaliation in favor of forgiveness. It is recited billions of times each day all over the world. We can lament that so ancient a prayer affirming a rejection of retaliation has not yet taken effect on the world stage—or even fully in our personal relationships.

Along these lines, here is a life-changing statement by Venerable Ghosananda, a Buddhist Patriarch of Cambodia. He shows us so clearly that letting go of the will to retaliate increases our capacity to love:

> I do not question that loving one's oppressors—Cambodians loving the Khmer Rouge—may be the most difficult attitude to achieve. But it is a law of the universe that retaliation, hatred, and revenge only continue the cycle and never stop it. Reconciliation does not mean that we surrender rights and conditions, but rather . . . it means that we see ourselves in the opponent—for what is the opponent but being in ignorance, and we ourselves are also ignorant of many things. Therefore, only loving kindness and right mindfulness can free us.[2]

The patriarch's declaration summarizes and highlights the nature of a spirituality of nonviolence. Commitment to nonviolence is a sweeping innovation, a subversive way of relating. The Patriarch's words present a far-reaching manifesto of what mature human goodness really is. We realize: "I love my enemy when my response to his arrows is meant to relieve him of the suffering in him that led to his being hurtful, aggressive, and oppressive toward me."

WHEN HATE HAPPENS

Revenge is fueled by hate. Hate is *holding on* to blame, ill will, resentment, and retaliation. Its definition is the opposite of that of forgiveness: a *letting go* of blame, ill will, resentment, and retaliation. Forgiveness frees us and grants closure after a painful event. Hate stays in us, eats away at us. The rage, blame, and venomous ill will are unceasing. Our revenges are ongoing; our need to hurt back is insatiable. There is no "this revenge has gone far enough." In hate the need to hurt is never used up.

Satan, in John Milton's *Paradise Lost*, book 4, says:

For never can true reconcilement grow
Where wounds of deadly hate have pierced so deep: . . .
All hope excluded thus. . . .[3]

When we hate we do not seek reconcilement with an offender.
Nor do we want or accept compunction in the offender. We will
not be satisfied with an apology. We do not want reconnection,
just ongoing punishment. We also lose any chance of having hope
in humanity, which is a path to the revoking of hate. Hate-fueled
vengeance is a frequent style among street gangs whose members are wounded in so many sad, unreconciled ways that are the
breeding ground for retaliatory egos. Among them, there is no
chance for the offender to make up for an offense, there is only
room for vengeance, usually in the form of physical attack. The
offender has only one option: pay, not make it okay. We notice
that Milton sees hate as a *wound deep within us.* So much of our
need for revenge reflects and reveals how trauma affects us—in
the past and in the present.

Here is another example of exclusion. "Cancel culture" refers
to disapproval and social pressure that is meant to lead to firing
people or preventing them from continuing to pursue their ca-
reers or callings. We withdraw support, for instance, from public
figures or groups who have done what is considered politically
incorrect. Then ostracizing is often carried out on social media.
Such shaming is retaliatory. It is also an avoidance of dialogue
or asking for amends or compensation when appropriate. These
are alternatives that represent accountability with inclusion. We
see here the difference between people who seek reconciliation
and those who seek punishment, which in this instance is another
word for vengeance.

We can put energy into working toward a change of heart,
healing conflicts, and finding appropriate and kindly ways to gain
closure. We then welcome repentance from others, a turnabout

that leads to connection. Punishment leads only to disconnection, usually with a vengeful purpose. Healthy people want friendship restored; they want bygones to be bygones. They want repair and do all they can to get it to happen. Hate can't go there. This is why *healthy people might occasionally retaliate but they never hate.*

We might hate someone but not show it directly. For instance, a worker who hates his boss might be pleasant toward her so she will promote him or for fear she may not. He would like to retaliate, but he knows this will sabotage his chances for advancement, so he may even act obsequiously toward her. That style is not release from the cage of retaliation; it is simply a tactic for self-promotion. Another scenario in this example might be that the disgruntled worker does not want the boss to know of his anger, so he is passive-aggressive, doing what makes her look bad or spreading malicious rumors or gossip about her, which are forms of indirect retaliation.

People who love us may be mad at us but they won't or can't stay mad and soon forgive us. People who hate us can't stop being mad at us and won't forgive us, ever. Both love and hate can be permanent. The difference is that love survives on the healings of rifts while hate thrives on keeping wounds open. Holding on to hate toward someone is the equivalent of self-hate: we are impairing our minds with obsession, stunting our capacity for magnanimity, annulling our spiritual practices, and harming our body by an ongoing stress that affects our immune system and blood pressure. Life thrives only on love and the joy it bestows.

OUR THREE MAIN CHOICES WHEN OTHERS HATE US OR HURT OUR FEELINGS

Our discussion of hate reminds us of the given of life that people might hate us or hurt our feelings. Some people might hurt our feelings. Here is a summary glance at three of the choices available to us when hate or when hurt feelings happen to us.

A PRIMITIVE REACTION FROM WHAT IS CALLED OUR REPTILIAN BRAIN	A COMMITMENT TO "DO NO HARM" FROM OUR ETHICAL SENSE OF MORAL RESPONSIBILITY	AN EXPRESSION OF UNCONDITIONAL LOVING-KINDNESS FROM OUR SPIRITUAL CONSCIOUSNESS
We hurt or hate back.	We do not hurt or hate back.	We do not hurt or hate back. We go one step further and do good to those who hurt or hate us. This may include continuing contact or simply goodwill toward them, wishing them the best without further contact. In all this we hold an intention to forgive.
We pay back.	We do not pay back.	We love back.
We copy the other person.	We act in our own new way.	We show unconditional love.
We hear an avenger's voice: "Do it too."	We hear a mediator's voice: "Don't do it."	We hear Michelle Obama: "When they go low, we go high."[4]
We become aggressive, actively or passively. We retaliate to "right the wrong" in accord with street rules.	We act in accord with moral principles and a commitment to nonviolence. We take the moral high ground.	We act in accord with teachings such as the Sermon on the Mount, or the Buddhist practice of loving-kindness, or a generous version of the Golden Rule.

An adrenaline/ testosterone-driven ego-saving reaction of ill will	An oxytocin/heart-motivated respect for all people	An oxytocin-rich, open-hearted sense of human solidarity
Ego-based— i.e., fear-based	Humanism-based	Love-based
"I alone am important!"	"You are important too!"	"We are deeply linked!"
We give in to our dark side.	We show our love, caring, generosity, and compassion.	We open to a to grace that expands and deepens our commitment to love.
Win-lose	Win-win by two people	Win-win by two connected individuals
We are like the guys in the *Godfather* movies.	We are like Mr. Rogers or Atticus Finch.	We are Christ or Buddha in the world of today.
We enjoy the sweetness of revenge—i.e., the sense of power that we got back at the person/s who crossed us, and we are glad we can look good in the eyes of our gang.	We grow in self-respect because we remain true to our personal standards no matter how others behave. We have found something sweeter than revenge.	We love ourselves and all beings more, we move toward enlightenment/ transformation— and we want that for everyone.
We are followers.	We are heroes and heroines.	We are saints and bodhisattvas.
Our motivation is the promotion of our ego.	Our motivation is caring for the common good.	Our motivation is birthing a world of justice, peace, and love.

A PRIMITIVE REACTION FROM WHAT IS CALLED OUR REPTILIAN BRAIN	A COMMITMENT TO "DO NO HARM" FROM OUR ETHICAL SENSE OF MORAL RESPONSIBILITY	AN EXPRESSION OF UNCONDITIONAL LOVING-KINDNESS FROM OUR SPIRITUAL CONSCIOUSNESS
This natural reaction takes no special effort.	This response takes a change in attitude.	This response takes inner work and follow-up action.
Intimacy cannot happen. We lose the opportunity for healthy intimate connection.	Intimacy can happen. We open to the opportunity for intimate connection and conflict resolution.	Intimacy deepens and flourishes. We increase the opportunities for intimate connection between all beings and provide a healthy model for others.

The far-left column presents behavior that seems warranted and righteous and that we might expect to happen. The center column shows behavior that respects all people and is not expected to happen. The far-right column shows behavior that goes way beyond than what is expected and aligns with our highest consciousness to deepen and expand our relationships and our capacity for love.

The far-right column shows what a changeover from selfishness to selflessness looks like. Using religious terminology, such transformation is a conversion—that is, an inner and outer turnabout activated by transformative grace. It moves us from self-preoccupation to love, the self-surrender that is ego loss and heart gain. Our surrender is an interior event, something that happens inside us, making us love people and the earth with the heart of the universe. This gigantic and joyous opening in us wants to happen, and all we have to do is say *yes*. The welcome result, so welcome, is that we become wholeheartedly human.

We have all heard the recommendation: "Kill him with kindness." This is not what the third column refers to. That is the ego's way to show off its rank "above" the offender. In sincere spiritual consciousness, our nonviolent response to offenses is about showing how spiritually advanced we are. Nor is it a spiritual practice to act kindly in order to show others how primitive they are compared to us. Elitism is the ego's way, not the heart's way.

The recommendation that we do good and show forgiving love to those who have offended us is definitely an over-the-top, counterintuitive style. We do more than forgo retaliation. We take a giant step of saintliness and do something that will benefit those who have harmed us. We see an example of this style in *Les Misérables* by Victor Hugo. Bishop Myriel kindly hosts Jean Valjean, who steals his household silver and runs off. The police capture Jean, but the bishop tells them that he *gave* the silver to Jean and even offers Jean silver pieces he had left behind. Bishop Myriel gives a desperate homeless man a chance to set himself up in business rather than be put into prison. We notice in this story that the practice of unstinting magnanimity is essential if we are to show unconditional loving-kindness, doing good to those who hate or hurt us. This generosity, in religion, is a virtue. Generosity in Buddhism is the first perfection of an enlightened life. Such generosity is not limited to the giving of money. Spiritually aware generosity is ultimately about sharing in an unconditional, unreserved, universal, and unending practice of loving-kindness toward all beings.

Here is a modern example of a choice for living from that spiritual consciousness: the parents of a son killed by a drunk driver put energy into rehabilitating the driver once he is released from prison. A tragic event has transformed those who are left behind—and they hope it transforms the offender too. Anyone can act this way once the impulse to retaliate has surrendered to the urge to renovate. Transformed ourselves, we now wish transformation, not suffering, for those who have hurt us or anyone. Shantideva, in *The Way of the Bodhisattva*, states this lofty spiritual style in such a touching way:

> May those whose hell it is
> To hate and hurt
> Be turned into lovers
> Bringing flowers.

TECHNOLOGIES FOR CHANGE

Spiritual practices are our technologies for across-the-board change in our habits, attitudes, values, world views, priorities, ambitions, and hearts. In our transformed state, we would never say: "Living well is the best revenge." We don't want the "sweetness" of revenge in any form. "Living well" is a life of nonretaliation, a life of loving-kindness: "I am living well because I no longer have to retaliate." A true change in us installs a whole new mindset, one that sees no appeal at all in making sure the one who hurt us notices we are now better off.

Any transformation combines an ending and a beginning. Transformation takes a journey of inner work and new outer behavior. Thus, a commitment to going beyond retaliation may take a hefty remodel of our ambitions and actions. We will brazenly instate a new life program that is designed not by ego but by alignment to the highest potentials in us: letting go of egotism and showing unconditional love and the virtue of forgivingness. We will then find the freedom that comes from adopting a new life motto: "From ego habits to loving choices. From payback to love back." Transformations herald an end to our long human love affair with revenge.

In our new way of living, we give up our attachment to ego status. We refuse to retaliate even when it is expected of us.

We also endure shaming from those who see us as cowards for choosing a nonretaliatory alternative. Our commitment is no longer to play the game of defending our delicately poised ego: we walk off the field, unaffected by the jeers of our teammates. Yes, we may expect a judgment by others when we act in such a surprising way. After all, we are being disloyal to the primitive code of payback. We are not abiding by the tribal rules of the game. We are losing our group identity in favor of a new identity, one that may isolate us. This is why letting go of ego status takes enormous courage. It is also why living in accord with our conscience can be lonely.

To move away from either the street or the gang mentality is to live by a code of newly defined honor, perhaps in a new circle of friends, certainly in a new lifestyle, with a new set of values, a new mindset, and, most importantly, with a newly formed conscience. We are no longer intent on conforming to social requirements and strictures. In other words, we have become uninhibited.

This is a lot like what happens to us in recovery from an addiction, only this time the addiction is to society's opinion and its standards. In a recovery program we turn to a power greater than that of ego. That power redefines honor and supports us in becoming champions at letting go of retaliation. The result is a world of justice, peace, and love, which we were given a lifetime to cocreate. They become the three goals we work for in society. But they are also three qualities of our own enlightened nature, a universe within. We are not searching for justice, peace, and love, we are locating what we already and always have and are, what is never really lost.

Finally, going beyond retaliation is a spiritual practice fully in keeping with the program of restorative rather than retributive justice that we may see in a court setting. We can say that spiritual practitioners of nonretaliation support restorative justice in the courts, seeing it as a giant step in the right direction. What makes something a spiritual practice is that it transforms all areas of human life and relationships. Here is an example. A lawyer who stands for restorative justice may at the same time retaliate against her wife. A lawyer with a spiritual practice, however, extends her program from court to home to world. A life commitment is a life transformation.

A NOTE FROM BEN

Benjamin Franklin made a recommendation regarding revenge in *Poor Richard's Almanac* and in *Familiar Letters*: "*Doing* an Injury puts you below your Enemy; *Revenging* one makes you but *even* with him; *Forgiving* it sets you *above* him."[5] In the first clause, Ben laments that we wind up one-down. In the second clause Ben asserts that revenge will not go far enough; it will make us "even." In the final clause, he states that forgiveness "sets you above." The forgiveness itself is certainly commendable. But, Ben, look at the motivation you propose: one-upmanship rather than compassion and equality, what we all really long for when we live from the heart. Instead, you suggest that we forgive someone because that will set us "above him." The whole recommendation puts the wounded ego back on its throne! And it won't be long before the enemy-turned-victim, feeling patronized and perhaps embarrassed, will become our persecutor. And the whole, or rather, unwholesome, story perpetuates itself.

Ben Franklin is an icon of humanist wisdom, what helps us live sanely and cooperatively. But that wisdom does not produce the full set of ingredients that make for human wholeness. In mature spiritual consciousness we are out for higher stakes—that is, living lovingly no matter what others may do. In that world there is no below or above. We are already and always even. We have come to see all beings as on an equal plane. We sound a higher note in the symphony of humanness: "Love your enemies." We live by the following poem:

He drew a circle that shut me out—
Heretic, rebel, a thing to flout.
But Love and I had the wit to win:
We drew a circle that took him in![6]

—Edwin Markham, "Outwitted"

NINE

Why Turn the Other Cheek?

MOST RELIGIONS SEE REVENGE as wrong. Hardly any religion specifically broadcasts it as a commandment. The Sermon on the Mount—the main Christian teaching on letting go of retaliation, the main influence on Gandhi regarding nonviolent resistance—is considered by the church to be a counsel, not a commandment. In other words, it is a recommendation but not a requirement for the ultimate goal of personal salvation. In most religions adhering to the commandments makes for salvation. Adhering to the Sermon on the Mount makes for sanctity, which is the style of those who want to go one step beyond what is necessary and embrace what is heroic.

The saints, religious or otherwise, who followed the path of nonviolence were the exceptions in history, not the rule. This is the realization that led me to believe that a full commitment to going beyond retaliation, no matter what the cost, requires a special awakening, a grace of radical transformation. Here are two examples of what is meant by the rarity of a special calling: There were several ministers ordained with Martin Luther King Jr., but only he taught indefatigably about the value of nonviolence and then died in its cause. There were many slavers in the eighteenth century, but only the slaver John Newton could write "Amazing Grace," the song commemorating his conversion to a conscientious objection to slavery.

In any case, it is certain that many were called to join the Christian religion over the centuries, but few were chosen to uphold nonretaliation as a full-on commitment. We also notice that only a minority of religious leaders or teachers over the centuries pointed to revenge as wrong. Likewise, many people over the ages have been notional adherents to religious moral teachings. But only a few have displayed an awakened conscience regarding the active letting go of retaliation as a necessary practice on the spiritual path.

In my own musing on this topic, I wondered how many of the early Christian writers truly got it that revenge is not the way of Christ. I noticed the paucity of references in the New Testament to transcending payback. Several years ago, I read the Book of Acts, which describes the early experiences and teachings of the apostles. I read it word for word with one specific purpose in mind: to find out how many of the believers definitely and fully embraced the teaching of letting go of retaliation. I found only one clear example of someone—St. Stephen—who really got the nonretaliatory, full forgiveness message: "They [those executing him for his Christian beliefs] went on stoning Stephen as he called on the Lord and said, 'Lord Jesus, receive my spirit!' Then falling on his knees, he cried out with a loud voice, 'Lord, do not hold this sin against them!'" (Acts 7:59–60).

Here are other New Testament passages that show an inconsistency about the moral value of nonretaliation. In Luke 23, Jesus, dying on the cross between two criminals, is treated with scorn by one and with kindness by the other. The story has Jesus welcome only the faithful one into his heavenly kingdom: "Today you [singular] will be with me in paradise." In fully going beyond retaliation the words to the two malefactors might instead have been "You will both be with me today in paradise. I take you, faithful man, out of appreciation. I take you, scornful man, out of compassion." This would have reflected the same unconditional forgiveness as in Jesus's following words: "Father forgive them [all]." The selective reward to the "good" person and punishment of the "bad" person does not coincide with Christ's unconditionally merciful style in the Sermon on the Mount: "Love your enemies. . . . Do [them all] good."

Another example appears in Luke 16:19–31, the story of the starving Lazarus and the rich man who refused to give him food. Eternal torture is the rich man's punishment. Lazarus, who once was poor, is given the riches of heaven. Lazarus, out of compassion, would have helped his oppressor who was calling to him from hell, but God prevents that. Not a drop of water is allowed the burning man, since he is getting his just desserts.

The story of the prodigal son, Luke 15:11–32, shows a compassionate alternative. The father forgives his wastrel son before even fully hearing his confession of guilt and repentance. We see another clear understanding of letting go of retaliation in the First Letter of Peter: "He [Jesus] was insulted and did not retaliate with insult; he was tortured and made no threat" (2:23). The importance of letting go of retaliation in favor of reconciliation comes through in this passage from St. Paul: "God was reconciling the world to himself in Christ, not counting people's sins against them. And he has committed to us the message of reconciliation" (2 Corinthians 5:18–19).

We also might find it confusing that the God in the Sermon on the Mount is not the same as the God who said: "Vengeance is mine; I will repay" (Deuteronomy 32:35). Instead, this God loves his enemies. This is shown in the fact that he "makes the sun rise on the evil and the good, the rain [fall] on the unjust and the just" (Matthew 5:45). The Roman philosopher Seneca, in *On Benefits*, reflects that same lofty teaching: "If you are imitating the gods, confer benefits on the ungrateful too; for the sun rises for criminals too and the seas are open even to pirates."[1] These two quotations, taken together, show us what the Sermon calls us to do, or rather, to be.

Along these lines, Kurt Vonnegut, in *A Man Without a Country*, wrote:

> For some reason, the most vocal Christians among us never mention the Beatitudes. But, often with tears in their eyes, they demand that the Ten Commandments be posted in public buildings. And of course that's Moses, not Jesus. I haven't heard one of them demand that the Sermon on the Mount, the Beatitudes, be posted anywhere.
>
> "Blessed are the merciful" in a courtroom? "Blessed are the peacemakers" in the Pentagon? Give me a break![2]

Kurt Vonnegut asks us to question ourselves: Do we live by a tribal code that forces us to restore injured honor—that is, to salve our bruised ego by retaliation?

In summation, we can say that insistence on revenge is certainly contrary to the heartfelt teachings in the Sermon on the Mount. Ratifying or engaging in revenge does not align with mature spiritual consciousness in any context. On the other hand, not every human can be expected to have mature spiritual consciousness. We can see why showing full allegiance to a life of nonviolence remains a special calling and takes extensive practice to fulfill. Look at the contradictory conundrum embedded in humankind's struggle to survive: Letting go of retaliation is humanity's calling if it is to survive. But not everyone can be expected to embrace it. For humankind to survive we would all have to follow a special calling, and that is not possible. This is why history sometimes frightens us, and universal love is still only a possibility of possibilities.

TURNING THE OTHER CHEEK

The Sermon famously suggests turning the other cheek. In biblical times a slap to the face was a scornful insult, and a backhand slap was considered more contemptuous than a forehand slap. The left hand was used for cleanup after defecation, so a lefthanded slap added a further level of insult.

Jesus does not recommend turning the other cheek to spite the other or show him we are unfazed. That can be a sign of passive-aggression, another form of retaliation. Giving up retaliation is giving up that form of power and with it the importance of saving face. We are thereby asserting a new capacity, a Sermon on the Mount–formed conscience in the face of an abuser. Now reciprocity means love back in kindness, not pay back in kind.

However, when turning the other cheek means allowing an abuser to continue abusing us, it is not a healthy spiritual practice. By enduring and opening to more abuse we are encouraging and enabling someone to be unjust toward us and others. Such acceptance of violence may likely increase the abuser's aggression. It also legitimates abuse in all relationships. From this perspective, the precept "turn the other cheek" cannot be taken as an absolute. It can, however, be part of nonviolent action on a collective level, as it was for Gandhi's followers. Then it is symbolic of the seriousness of an oppressed group's confrontation with injustice. Likewise, turning the other cheek can become a symbol of nonviolent resistance. Of course it only communicates that if the abuser understands the significance of our gesture.

Modern biblical scholarship, by the way, shows that every word of the Sermon on the Mount is from the Hebrew Bible and rabbinical teaching. It is not new information from Jesus. The Sermon simply pulls ancient teachings on nonviolence into one document, one that is Judeo-Christian.

HOSPITALITY TO TWO
SIDES OF OURSELVES

When the Sermon on the Mount is entirely about transformation, it presents us with a challenging spiritual practice: only and always act with pure love. We no longer even consider the distinction between counsel and commandment. We simply love one another. This will take a combination of firm courage and tender guilelessness. Jesus made a recommendation regarding these two possibilities: "Behold, I am sending you out as lambs among wolves; therefore be as shrewd as serpents and as guileless as doves" (Matthew 10:16).

There is very little hope for us if we are only vulnerable lambs facing a power that does not want to work something out with us but to destroy us. Yet the second half of the verse tells us that we don't have to lose hope when we are outmatched. We don't have to be fearful about engaging in the battle, no matter the odds. We will gain strength through our spiritual commitment—in this case, to combine shrewdness and gentleness.

The word *serpents* in Jesus's recommendation, reminding us that the devil first appeared in the Bible as a serpent, tells us that the evil referred to is not garden-variety (pun intended) nastiness; rather, it can be brutal and demonic. Yet we can act with the shrewdness of a demon and join it to our own commitment to guilelessness. So we combine serpentlike shadow energy with dovelike nonviolent energy, and an existential hope arises from that combination. We might also say that it is the very combining of these opposites that invariably evokes hope in humanity. It is how we survive the shadow and transmute its energy from negative/useless to positive/useful. We don't kill the wolves; we convert them to guard dogs.

Only a combination of opposites will make for a true spiritual practice. Now two opposites collapse into one splendid result. Notice that Jesus does not offer a promise, only a practice. In any case, there will never be only love or only peace, but there can be more love than before we got here and more peace because we stayed here practicing peace and love. There will also never be total freedom from fear, but there can be less fear in us when we don't back down.

Indeed, our spiritual practices do not promise safety or success. They are standards meant to renovate society and benefit all beings, which is the ultimate purpose of the Sermon on the Mount and the life of Buddha, Jesus, and of all of us.

Finally, here is an example of the joining of shrewd and gentle capacities at an international level. In 1979, after years of border disputes, Ecuador and Peru signed a treaty regarding debated turf. Part of the treaty created a binational park, the Cordillera del Condor. Now the border clashes have ceased and both countries can enjoy a protected land. Opposing sides found a way to benefit from the land equally rather than go to war over it.

MY OWN STORY

My interest in the moral option beyond revenge began in the seminary on the day we were studying the Sermon on the Mount in scripture class. The professor told us not to take any of it literally. I dismissed that as too facile. I knew it was meant to be taken seriously by anyone responsive to a spiritual calling. I also knew I wasn't following it in my daily life. What bothered me most that day was my strong reaction to the Sermon. I disliked the whole concept of "turning the other cheek" rather than indulging in reprisals. Yet I knew the teaching was essential to being a Christian and I wanted to be that.

I knew no one could help me parse this personal negative reaction. So I decided on my own to write out the whole Sermon longhand, over and over, until I figured out what I was so fiercely opposing. I sat at my desk that very night and began writing. About halfway through, my head popped up from the page and I said to myself aloud: "Jesus wants to take away my ego!" By "ego" I meant entitlement to retaliation in this unfair, cruel world. Indeed, for me, from childhood on, retaliation was not only a recommendation—it was a sacrament. Not to get back at those who offended me was nothing less than cowardice. My definition of power was not that of Christ but of the entitled, arrogant, controlling street-gang ego, pure and simple. That realization was the beginning of my seeing the importance of letting go of retaliation.

But it was a change happening only in my mind. I went right on retaliating consciously and unconsciously. My revenges only ended on a miraculous day in 1991 when my friend Louie took me to a Chinese Buddhist temple in New York state and I stood alone before a statue of the Buddha in a silent heart-to-heart moment. I found myself looking into the eyes of this Buddha and feeling a transformation of heart because of what must have been a grace from his heart. I had not planned to make a vow. I had not even thought about retaliation beforehand. I just heard myself suddenly say exactly this to Buddha: "I vow never again to knowingly retaliate." The words flowed out with no planning or even volition. The vow made itself, as only the best vows do. Buddha nature graced me. I was, without argument, letting go of the intention to retaliate.

In that moment I was also, though I did not realize this until years later, trusting the Buddha nature of all beings. My vow to forgive rather than retaliate is a way of acknowledging the inherent goodness in all beings. My vow also shows that I am trusting Buddha nature in others to emerge when I forgive. So both of us benefit: I display Buddha nature and so does the other person. That makes forgiveness the real miracle.

Only recently, thanks to these words of Joan Halifax, did I begin to appreciate what was really going on that day in New York: "What are we vowing, other than to be who we really are?" The

David beyond the ego version of David made a vow to be born. That was the first day of my life beyond retaliation. As far as I know, I have never broken my vow, thanks to the power of grace, the gift dimension of the universe that had found a path to me. On that day, I knew my calling was real and that there would be no going back to my reptilian-style of living. I also knew I had been deputed, as a writer and teacher, not only to change myself but to share my experience. What I have been sharing in all my books and talks and now fully in these pages is how to find spiritual alternatives to payback. And this remains my calling.

I don't feel like a saint or better than anyone else. All that has happened is that now I like myself more and feel immensely thankful. By a spiritual alchemy I found such a precious lively gift, my true nature, in the ruins of my stubborn ego.

I was twenty-four that night in the seminary. I was fifty-one that day in the temple. Yes, it took that long. I realize now that my age had a lot to do with my clinging to payback as a sign of strength. I gave a talk to a Buddhist group last week. There were three young men in the group of mostly older people that made up the sangha. Each of them, and only them, objected strongly to my message about letting go of retaliation in personal relationships. They protested that such a commitment would mean giving up their power. I recalled having had that same belief and fear when I was their age. I knew there was no hope in convincing them in words about what can only happen by grace and time. I did not argue. I simply proposed that they consider that the dictionary definition of the word *power* is not the same as the Buddhist definition of it. I suggested that there was a new kind of power in a commitment to finding nonviolent solutions and in showing forgiveness. It is the power that happens in us when we live by a different standard from that of the rest of the world. It is the power of taking a stand for loving-kindness no matter who may label that as weakness.

Later I did a loving-kindness practice on my own for them, praying they let the light shine in, or rather, shine through, since the light is in all of us. I could not convince the young participants in my audience, but I think they did notice my joyful countenance now that I am free of acting in accord with the values of our mutual primitive ancestry. And my aspirations and prayers for their, and all the world's, move toward loving-kindness are my best contribution to them now.

SOME HUMOR

At an agency where I used to work, there was a poster showing how to do CPR, cardiopulmonary resuscitation. I looked at it often and thought after a while that I now knew how to perform the procedure. Then one day, on closer look, I noticed the small print at the bottom of the poster: "CPR can't be learned from a poster." The ironic humor was balanced by my own sense of being gently tricked. In any case, the analogy applies to the topic of this book. We need more than a book to make a full commitment to going beyond retaliation. We need a long-held practice of loving-kindness. We need the assisting force of a higher power— Buddha, Christ, or universe. And all this happens in us because something has happened to us, not because something has been learned by us.

I share one more humorous experience along these lines. I have been teaching over the years, as in this book, that transformation and commitment to a practice of going beyond retaliation happens by grace. But recently I had to study the traffic laws of California in order to renew my driver's license. One section in the study guide made me a laugh at myself: "Signal an oncoming driver to shut off his high beams by flashing yours twice. If the other driver does not lower his high beams, do not retaliate by putting yours on. Simply proceed with no further action." In other words, according to the DMV, anyone, even someone without spiritual consciousness, can choose not to retaliate. I certainly agree. It is required by law, at least behind the wheel—dare we say the wheel of fortune?

In any case, as we see in the practices in this book, we don't have to wait to be touched by a higher power than the ego, we can "act as if" we had been graced by it right now. (*Act* in this context does not mean pretend or perform, but practice.)

Here is my best-stated view: a lifelong commitment to non-violence takes a special grace but we can act in nonviolent or nonretaliatory ways anytime, simply by choice. As we have been seeing throughout this book, our practice does not have to have a calling behind it. Our actions do not even have to have a spiritual dimension—but that may come with practice and openness to spiritual and saintly alternatives.

One important realization and question came to me recently. We might also give up retaliation and move toward forgivingness just because of our own bigheartedness. But isn't bigheartedness itself a gift?

PRACTICE

Affirmations of Freedom from Retaliation

Here are some affirmations based on the recommendations throughout this book. They can help raise our consciousness and keep us alert about letting go of our retaliatory behaviors. We state them aloud or internally as if they were already true of us. By also practicing what they declare, they come true.

I forgo payback; I love back.
I forgive those who trespass against me.
I am changing in myself what I want to see changed in others.
I give up the need to get even.

I am committed to letting go of retaliating.

I am joyous and thankful to have embarked on this gentle path.

I am thankful to be able to stay on this path a day at a time. I ask for the grace to do so every day from now on.

My commitment to nonviolent love is the standard I live by, irrespective of what others may do or how they act.

When people apologize, I am a thankful witness.

When people do not apologize, I am a compassionate witness.

May I do good to those who hate me, bless those who curse me, and pray for or wish enlightenment for those who have mistreated me.

May I let the light in and through me more and more.

May I show loving-kindness and magnanimity toward all beings.

May I show compassion to everyone who suffers—including myself.

May I be joyful about the good things that happen to any of us.

May I respond with equanimity, serenity, and courage to all that happens to me today.

May my love increase with every tomorrow.

May I always have a sense of humor.

May all these affirmations become commitments to a life of love.

May they come alive in this world still so lost in actions, policies, and wars of revenge.

May I always believe that there's still time.

A Daily Loving-Kindness Affirmation
I say Yes to everything that happens to me today
as an opportunity
to give and receive love and to free myself from fear.
I am thankful for the enduring capacity to love
that has come to me from the
Sacred Heart of the universe.
May everything that happens to me today
open my heart more and more.
May all that I think, say, feel, do, and am
express loving-kindness
toward myself, those close to me, and all beings.
May love be my life purpose, my bliss,
my destiny, my calling,
the richest grace I can receive or give.
And may I always be compassionate
toward people who are considered
least or last or who feel alone or lost.
May all of us cocreate
a world of justice, peace, and love.

Epilogue

AT THE THRESHOLD

This book does not come to an end but to a threshold. At a threshold we look both back and ahead. We look back at what we have read in this book and forward to any changes we see ourselves considering or making based on it. Maybe we will find a new world, within and around us. All beings may become the population of our spiritual community, our circumference-less circle of loving-kindness. We then find ourselves trusting the inherent goodness in everyone. Abraham Lincoln, in his "Second Inaugural Address," trusted this possibility of spiritual conversion in all humans: "We [North and South] are not enemies, but friends. We must not be enemies. . . . The mystic chords of memory, stretching from every battlefield and patriot grave to every living heart and hearthstone over this broad land, will yet swell the chorus of the Union, when again touched, as surely they will be, by the better angels of our nature."[1] Letting go of ego and living by love are how those angels learn to fly.

In the Udana, a Buddhist scripture, we see the theme: "Those who love themselves will never harm others." The spiritual practice of nonretaliation is also a threshold into healthy self-love. We have come to care more about our own hearts. We want them to be networks of love for others, irrespective of how they have treated us. And we love ourselves for being that way. We also feel good about our transformation because we have found and followed a rare and interiorly rewarding spiritual path.

We grow in self-respect as we behold the stability of our commitment to going beyond retaliation. In other words, our standards apply and support us in unpleasant encounters. We see an example of this practice in the 1962 film *To Kill a Mockingbird*. Villainous Bob Ewell spits in the face of the hero Atticus Finch. Watching the film I immediately thought of what I was taught: a real man has to spit back and then punch him in the nose. This retaliatory response would be especially important since Atticus's young son was watching and would have to learn from his dad how a real man is supposed to act. But my childhood film hero, Gregory Peck, did not retaliate. He maintained eye contact with the offender, took out a handkerchief, and wiped off the spit in silence. The ego's need to retaliate did not have to define manhood. That is what is meant by a transformation from ego self to Buddha nature. That is how the spiritual practice supports us in moments of conflict. No longer subject to street rules, we welcome the personal appearance of our true nature, the One that is only and always going beyond retaliation.

In this book we have looked together into how revenge may be a part of our behavior and how to adopt an alternative spiritual path. The main path is the daily practice of loving-kindness in all our dealings, which is the central alternative to vengeance. My writing led me to three new aspirations that I have added to my own daily practice. I offer them to you, fellow practitioners, in case you might want to do the same. Reciting this even once will also be a hearty step into loving-kindness.

May anyone who has ever hated, harmed,
hurt my feelings, betrayed, or offended me in any
way find happiness, practice loving-kindness,
and become enlightened.

May anyone who will ever hate, harm, hurt my feelings, betray, or offend me in any way find happiness, practice loving-kindness, and become enlightened. May I and all beings who have sought revenge find happiness and practice loving-kindness on our path to enlightenment.

Appendix

QUOTATIONS FOR MEDITATION

Keep struggling for justice instead of taking revenge.
—Core teaching of the *Mahabharata*, a Hindu scripture

Hate does not cease by hate, only by love.
—Core teaching of the *Dhammapada*, a compilation of Buddhist teachings

One act of retaliation burns to the ground a whole forest of merit.
—Core teaching of the *Bequeathed Teachings Sutra*

When you are hurt but do not hurt back, you are a true victor.
—Core teaching of the *Sutra of Forty-Two Chapters*

When love is my only defense, I am invincible . . . Do good to the one who has injured you.
—Core teaching of the *Tao Te Ching*

Forgive your neighbor the wrongs he has done, and then your sins will be pardoned when you pray.
—Sirach 28:2

[God says to Israel]: "I will not remember your sins."
—Isaiah 43:25

. . . we forgive those who trespass against us.
—Matthew 6:12

Love your enemies, do good to those who hate you, bless those who curse you, pray for those who mistreat you.
—Luke 6:27–28

Do not take revenge, my dear friends . . . Do not be overcome by evil, but overcome evil with good.
—Romans 12:21

He did but see
The flatness of my misery, yet with eyes
Of pity, not revenge.[1]
—Shakespeare, *A Winter's Tale*

Nevertheless, we cannot allow our feelings of resentment to become so excessive that they altogether extinguish natural feelings of disinterested benevolence that we should have towards all people, even our hated enemies. Nor can we allow resentment to result in unjust behavior against our wrongdoers in terms of personal retaliation and revenge.[2]
—Sermon of Bishop Joseph Butler (1692–1752)

To turn all that we possess into the channel of universal love becomes the business of our lives.[3]
—John Woolman, Quaker abolitionist

Remember that nations do not die; humbled and oppressed, they chafe under the yoke imposed upon them, preparing a renewal of the combat, and passing down from generation to generation a mournful heritage of hatred and revenge.[4]
—Pope Benedict XV to the Allied powers at the end of World War I

O God, remember not only the men and women of good will but also those of ill will. But do not remember only the suffering they have inflicted on us. Remember the fruits we bought thanks to this suffering: our comradeship, our loyalty, our humility, and the courage, generosity, and greatness of heart that has grown out of all this. And when they come to judgment let all the fruits we have borne become their forgiveness.
—Found at the women's concentration camp at Ravensbrück, 1945

The enemy must be resisted in so far as he serves the power of darkness, although it would be better to say that the power of darkness should be resisted rather than the enemy. He should be seen not as the servant of darkness but as someone who is capable of a future conversion. Therefore, though he uses evil means—despotism, the sword, force, darkness—one must not answer him with these same means. If one answers him in kind, with lies, deceit, violence and force, one would be denying oneself and him the future and the possibility of change, one would be perpetuating the kingdom of evil.[5]
—Milan Machoveč, A Marxist Looks at Jesus

To feel compassion for evildoers is not to condone the evil they commit. It is to yearn that they be free of the impulses that compel them to behave in such harmful ways, and thereby be free of the causes of suffering.[6]

—B. Alan Wallace, *Contemplative Science: Where Buddhism and Neuroscience Converge*

Violence simply is not radical enough, since it generally changes only the rulers but not the rules. What use is a revolution that fails to address the fundamental problem: the existence of domination in all its forms, and the myth of redemptive violence that perpetuates it?[7]

—Walter Wink, *Jesus and Nonviolence: A Third Way*

Sooner or later all the people of the world will have to discover a way to live together in peace, and thereby transform this pending cosmic elegy into a creative psalm of brotherhood. If this is to be achieved, man must evolve for all human conflict a method which rejects revenge, aggression and retaliation. The foundation of such a method is love.[8]

—Dr. Martin Luther King Jr.

Too often we honor swagger and bluster and the wielders of force; too often we excuse those who are willing to build their own lives on the shattered dreams of others. Some Americans who preach nonviolence abroad fail to practice it here at home. Some who accuse others of inciting riots have by their own conduct invited them.[9]

—Robert F. Kennedy, "On the Mindless Menace of Violence," a speech given at the City Club of Cleveland on April 5, 1968, the day after the Rev. Martin Luther King Jr. was assassinated in Memphis

By our nonviolent action we shall show that truth has its own strength.[10]

—Danilo Dolci, Italian social activist and poet

The history of vengeance committed in the name of God is not a function of any one religion but of the union of religious and political power. It is one of the great paradoxes of religious history that sacred injunctions designed to contain the worst impulses of men and women have, when wedded to secular power, so often been vehicles to express those very passions. . . . The Christianity preached by Jesus makes abandonment of vengeance a condition of personal salvation; the Christianity expounded by ecclesiastical authority has, at many points in history, made vindictiveness a condition of institutional survival.[11]

—Susan Jacoby, *Wild Justice: The Evolution of Revenge*

WHEN NONVIOLENCE AND NONRETALIATION PUT US IN HARM'S WAY

In self-defense that is nonretaliatory we balance vulnerability with self-care. There is, however, a special calling to some spiritually conscious people. It is *subjecting* themselves to suffering. Enduring suffering as a form of militant nonviolence requires a commitment that is unacceptable and frightening to most of us. Yet some spiritual practitioners choose this path. Here are some examples of this over-the-top style of heroes, martyrs, and saints who show a willingness to die for what they believe in.

Let them kill, despise, and beat [my body], / Using it according to their wish. / And though they treat it like a toy, / Or make of it the butt of every mockery, / My body has been given up to them. / Why should I make so much of it? . . . All those who slight me to my face / Or do to me some

other evil, / Even if they blame or slander me, / May they attain the fortune of enlightenment![12]
—Shantideva, *The Way of the Bodhisattva*

Even if bandits were to sever you savagely limb from limb with a two-handled saw . . . you should train thus: "Our minds will remain unaffected, and we shall utter no evil words; we shall abide in compassion for their welfare, with a mind of loving-kindness, without inner hate."[13]
—Bhikkhu Ñāṇamoli and Bhikkhu Bodhi, *The Middle Length Discourses of the Buddha: A Translation of the* Majjhima Nikāya

Whenever someone out of envy does me wrong by attacking or belittling me, I will take defeat upon myself, and give the victory to others. Even when someone . . . mistreats me very unjustly, I will view that person as a true spiritual teacher.[14]
—Geshe Langri Thangpa, "Eight Stanzas for Mind Training"

Let him give his cheek to the smiter, and be filled with insults.
—Lamentations 3:30

You have heard that it was said, "An eye for an eye and a tooth for a tooth." But I say to you, do not resist an evildoer. But if anyone strikes you on the right cheek, turn the other also; and if anyone wants to sue you and take your coat, let him have your cloak as well.
—Matthew 5:38–40

I appeal to you therefore, brothers and sisters, by the mercies of God, to present your bodies as a living sacrifice . . .
—Romans 12:1

I am the wheat of God, and let me be ground by the teeth of the wild beasts, that I may be found the pure bread of Christ.[15] [A reference to Christians thrown to lions in the Colosseum.]

—St. Ignatius of Antioch (died 107), "Letter to the Romans"

Time, force, and death,
Do to this body what extremes you can;
But the strong base and building of my love
Is as the very center of the earth,
Drawing all things to it.[16]
—Shakespeare, *Troilus and Cressida*

God sees the whole road. All I see is the step I am about to take. All I know is that I must get to God's heart. And if that way is through the flames, then behold through the flames I come.

—*The Passion of Joan of Arc*, 1928 French film

I seek entirely to blunt the edge of the tyrant's sword, not by putting up against it a sharper-edged weapon, but by disappointing his expectation that I would be offering physical resistance.

—Mahatma Gandhi, in *Young India*, August 10, 1935

We will take direct action against injustice despite the failure of governmental and other official agencies to act first. We will not obey unjust laws or submit to unjust practices. We will do this peacefully, openly, cheerfully because our aim is to persuade. We adopt the means of nonviolence because our end is a community at peace with itself. We will try to persuade with our words, but if our words fail, we will try to persuade with our acts. We will always be willing to talk and seek fair compromise, but we are ready to suffer when necessary and even to risk our lives to become witnesses to truth as we see it.[17]

—Dr. Martin Luther King Jr., "The Quest for Peace and Justice"

A STORY THAT POINTS TO THE PATH

Here is my version of a Zen story from Japanese Zen master Hakuin that I have been contemplating and retelling over the years. It pulls together our topics of finding wisdom and letting go of aggression.

Once upon a time in medieval Japan there was a violent and uncouth bandit who brutally ravaged the countryside. Yet though he was unschooled and certainly not known to be a philosopher, three questions continually plagued him and he fervently hoped that someone would answer them someday. He had heard that in the neighborhood he was now looting there was a monastery with a very wise abbot. Locating the monastery, without knocking and with no bows or salutations, the outlaw burst open the yew-wood door. There to his contented surprise he came face to face with the revered abbot.

The holy man was sitting on a mat in the lotus position meditating. He did not look up when the rude desperado, wild-eyed and putrid smelling, blurted out in a low Japanese rural dialect: "Teach me: what is hell, what is heaven, and what is enlightenment! Those are my three questions. I demand an answer right now—and it had better be good if you want to keep your head!"

The master, after a long minute of silence, looked up at the wreck of the desperado arching so fiercely over him. He replied with a grimace of scorn: "You are too stupid and thickheaded to understand subtle questions like those, let alone the answers.

So get out before I throw you out, body, reeking stench, shabby clothes, and all!"

Reeling with rage at this insult to his colossal ego and ready to slice off the offender's head, the bandit, ready for revenge, pulled his blood-stained sword from its scabbard. As he did so, the abbot pointed to the weapon and quietly commented: "That's hell." The bandit was suddenly dumbfounded, his startled countenance showing signs of bewilderment at the wisdom of the abbot's reply and disbelief that anyone could be this canny! He slowly slid his rapier back into its sheath and simultaneously the master pointed to the disappearing blade and gently added: "That's heaven." Now the eyes of the brigand filled with tears, and as his knees involuntarily bent to the ground he heard himself say: "I give up my life of crime and beg to be your most humble student." The abbot placed his hand on the head of his new pupil and murmured: "That's enlightenment."

Note the sequence in the bandit's transformation: from rage to revenge to gentling. We may also notice that the first words of the master were criticisms, rebukes meant to activate rage that he knew would be followed by revenge, the one-trick pony of the armed ego. The abbot was wise enough to know exactly how to disarm the ego and deftly convert the would-be student. He turned the questions into answers that had been demonstrated precisely by the bandit's behavior. The abbot showed how the answers were inside the bandit all along. The master was only the channel and mindful witness of the bandit's enlightenment. This story shows so touchingly the graced power of enlightenment to pierce the ego's primitive defenses and open the heart to its best defense—to defenselessness, the first door into the light.

NOTES

INTRODUCTION

1. William Shakespeare, *Richard III*, act 1, scene 2, accessed April 27, 2024, https://shakespeare.mit.edu/richardiii/full.html.
2. John Milton, *Paradise Lost*, ed. Michael Kaplan (New York: Barnes & Noble Classics, 2004), 9.171–72.

1. UNDERSTANDING RETALIATION

1. William Shakespeare, *Henry V*, act 2, scene 2, accessed April 27, 2024, https://shakespeare.mit.edu/henryv/henryv.2.2.html.
2. "Archie Is Branded," *All in the Family*, season 3, episode 20, directed by Bob LaHendro and John Rich, written by Vin Bogert, aired February 24, 1973, on CBS.
3. Charles Darwin, *The Descent of Man and Selection in Relation to Sex*, 2nd ed. (1874), 54. https://charles-darwin.classic-literature.co.uk/the-descent-of-man/ebook-page-54.asp.
4. Yuval Noah Harari, "'It's Time to Give Peace Another Chance': Thousands Rally in Tel Aviv to End the War," *Jerusalem Post*, July 2, 2024, https://www.jpost.com/israel-news/article-808656.
5. Jimmy Carter, "Losing My Religion for Equality," *The Age*, July 12, 2009, https://www.theage.com.au/national/losing-my-religion-for-equality-20090712-ge80.html.

6. Aeschylus, *Agamemnon*, trans. E. D. A. Morshead (Project Gutenberg of Australia, updated September 2011), https://gutenberg.net.au/ebooks07/0700021h.html#ai.

2. FINDING ANOTHER WAY

1. Dogen, *Dogen's Pure Standards for the Zen Community: A Translation of the Eihei Shingi*, trans. Taigen Daniel Leighton and Shohaku Okumura (Albany: State University of New York, 1996), 110.
2. My book *You Are Not What You Think: The Egoless Path to Self-Esteem and Generous Love* (Boston: Shambhala Publications, 2015) offers a version of this section and may be helpful for further exploration of the topic of relating to an egotist.

3. FEELINGS, TRIGGERS, AND TRAUMAS

1. Alcoholics Anonymous, *Alcoholics Anonymous: The Story of How Many Thousands of Men and Women Have Recovered from Alcoholism*, 4th ed. (New York: Alcoholics Anonymous World Services, 2013), 67.
2. Emily Dickinson, *The Complete Poems of Emily Dickinson*, ed. Thomas H. Johnson (Boston: Back Bay Books, 1976), 285.

4. WHEN RETALIATING BECOMES THE NORM

1. Plato, *Crito*, in *Century Readings in Ancient Classical and Modern European Literature*, ed. John W. Cunliffe and Grant Showerman (New York: Century Co., 1925), 192.
2. Aristotle, *Rhetoric*, ed. Lee Honeycutt, book 2, chapter 2, modified March 15, 2004, https://kairos.technorhetoric.net/stasis/2017/honeycutt/aristotle/rhet2-2.html.

3. Aristotle, *Rhetoric*, ed. J. H. Freese, book 1, chapter 9, accessed April 28, 2025, http://www.perseus.tufts.edu/hopper /text?doc=Perseus%3Atext%3A1999.01.0060%3Abook %3D1%3Achapter%3D9.

4. William Shakespeare, *Troilus and Cressida*, act 5, scene 10, accessed April 27, 2024, https://shakespeare.mit.edu/troilus _cressida/troilus_cressida.5.10.html.

5. Pedro Arrupe, SJ, *Men and Women for Others*, speech, Valencia, Spain, July 31, 1973, Ignatian Solidarity Network, https:// ignatiansolidarity.net/men-and-women-for-others-fr-pedro -arrupe-s-j/.

6. Friedrich Nietzsche, *Human, All Too Human: A Book for Free Spirits*, trans. Helen Zimmern (New York: Macmillan, 1924), 5.

5. WHY WE PUNISH

1. "'The Grave Responsibility of Justice': Justice Robert H. Jackson's Opening Statement at Nuremberg," National WWII Museum, November 20, 2020, https://www.national ww2museum.org/war/articles/robert-jackson-opening-statement -nuremberg.

2. Elie Wiesel, *One Generation After* (New York: Schocken Books, 1982), 40.

3. Stephen Bachelor, *Buddhism Without Beliefs: A Contemporary Guide to Awakening* (New York: Riverhead Books, 1998), 111.

4. Hilarion Alfeyey, *The Spiritual World of Isaac The Syrian*, vol. 175, Cistercian Studies Series (Minnesota: Liturgical Press, 2000), chapter 1.

5. Julian of Norwich, *Revelations of Divine Love*, trans. Grace Warrack (Christian Classics Ethereal Library, 1901), chapter 45, https://ccel.org/ccel/julian/revelations/revelations.xvi.ii.html.

6. Thérèse of Lisieux, letter 226 to Father Adolphe Roulland, May 9, 1897, in her *Correspondence*, Archives of the Carmel of Lisieux, accessed May 1, 2024, https://archives.carmeldelisieux.fr/en/correspondance/lt-226-au-p-roulland-9-mai-1897/.

7. Saint Augustine, *Letters*, The Works of Saint Augustine: A Translation for the 21st Century, ed. John E. Rotelle, trans. Roland Teske (New York: New City Press, 2001), 357, https://wesleyscholar.com/wp-content/uploads/2019/04/Augustine-Letters-1-99.pdf.

8. Richard Rohr, "God Is Good: Your Image of God Creates You," Center for Action and Contemplation, September 12, 2021, https://cac.org/daily-meditations/god-is-good-you-image-of-god-creates-you-2021-09-12/.

6. FORGIVENESS AND FORGIVINGNESS

1. Hannah Arendt, *The Human Condition*, 2nd ed. (Chicago: University of Chicago Press, 1998), 241.

2. William Shakespeare, *The Tempest*, act 5, scene 1, accessed April 27, 2024, https://shakespeare.mit.edu/tempest/tempest.5.1.html.

3. Sophocles, *Antigone*, trans. Dudley Fitts and Robert Fitzgerald, https://mthoyibi.wordpress.com/wp-content/uploads/2011/05/antigone_2.pdf.

4. Kazuaki Tanahashi, ed. *The Treasury of the True Dharma Eye: Zen Master Dogen's* Shobo Genzo, vol. 1 (Boston: Shambhala Publications, 2010), 94.

5. Paul Tillich, *The Eternal Now* (New York: Scribner, 1963), 32.

6. Martin Luther King Jr., *Strength to Love* (Minneapolis: Fortress Press, 2010), 33.

7. Brad Inwood, trans. *Seneca: Selected Philosophical Letters* (New York: Oxford University Press, 2007), 81.

7. LOVE AND REVENGE IN INTIMATE RELATIONSHIPS

1. St. Augustine, *Confessions,* trans. Henry Chadwick, Oxford World's Classics (Oxford: Oxford University Press, 2009), 35.

2. I have more on this topic in my book *How to Be an Adult in Love: Letting Love in Safely and Showing It Recklessly* (Boston: Shambhala Publications, 2013).

3. Gordon Clifford (lyricist) and Harry Barris (composer), "I Surrender, Dear," first performed by Gus Arnheim and His Cocoanut Grove Orchestra with Bing Crosby for the Victor label in 1931.

4. Satguru Sivaya Subramuniyaswami, "Revenge Is a Terrible Negative Force," *Hinduism Today,* July 1, 2002, https://www.hinduismtoday.com/magazine/july-august-september-2002/2002-07-revenge-is-a-terrible-negative-force/.

5. These lines are inspired by "The More Loving One" by W. H. Auden.

8. FROM PAYBACK TO LOVE BACK

1. Martin Luther King Jr., speech at Illinois Wesleyan University (1966), https://www.iwu.edu/mlk/page-5.html.

2. Maha Ghosananda, *Step by Step: Meditations on Wisdom and Compassion,* ed. Philip Edmonds and Jane Sharada Mahoney (California: Parallax Press, 1991), 69.

3. John Milton, *Paradise Lost* (New York: Barnes & Noble Classics), 4.98–105.

4. The goal in "go high" is to adhere to our personal standard of integrity, not to claim that we are better than other people.

5. "Poor Richard Improved, 1749," *Founders Online,* National Archives, https://founders.archives.gov/documents/Franklin/01-03-02-0143. Original source: *The Papers of Benjamin*

Franklin, vol. 3, January 1, 1745, through June 30, 1750, ed. Leonard W. Labaree (New Haven: Yale University Press, 1961), pp. 331–350.

6. Edwin Markham, *The Shoes of Happiness and Other Poems* (New York: Doubleday, Page and Company, 1919).

9. WHY TURN THE OTHER CHEEK?

1. Lucius Seneca, *On Benefits,* trans. Brad Inwood and Miriam Griffin (Chicago: University of Chicago Press, 2011), 102.

2. Kurt Vonnegut, *A Man Without a Country* (New York: Random House Trade Paperbacks, 2007), 98.

EPILOGUE: AT THE THRESHOLD

1. Abraham Lincoln, "First Inaugural Address of Abraham Lincoln" (March 4, 1861), Yale Law School Lillian Goldman Law Library, https://avalon.law.yale.edu/19th_century/lincoln1.asp.

APPENDIX: QUOTATIONS FOR MEDITATION

1. William Shakespeare, *A Winter's Tale,* Folger Shakespeare Library, accessed March 27, 2025, https://www.folger.edu /explore/shakespeares-works/the-winters-tale/read/3/2/.

2. Ernesto V. Garcia, "Bishop Butler on Forgiveness and Resentment," *Philosophers' Imprint* 11, no. 10 (2011): 7.

3. John Woolman, *The Journal of John Woolman* (Boston: Houghton, Osgood, 1879), 22, https://ccel.org/ccel/woolman /journal/journal.

4. Pope Benedict XV, *To the Peoples Now at War and to Their Rulers* (Rome: The Holy See, 1915), https://www.vatican.va /content/benedict-xv/en/apost_exhortations/documents/hf _ben-xv_exh_19150728_fummo-chiamati.pdf.

5. Milan Machoveč, *A Marxist Looks at Jesus* (Philadelphia: Fortress Press, 1976), 109.

6. B. Alan Wallace, *Contemplative Science: Where Buddhism and Neuroscience Converge* (New York: Columbia University Press, 2006), 121.

7. Walter Wink, *Jesus and Nonviolence: A Third Way* (Minneapolis: Fortress Press, 2003), 72–73.

8. Martin Luther King Jr., speech in acceptance of the Nobel Peace Prize (Oslo, Norway, December 10, 1964), https://www.nobelprize.org/prizes/peace/1964/king/acceptance-speech/.

9. Robert F. Kennedy, "Remarks to the Cleveland City Club" (April 5, 1968), recorded as a news release and collected in papers held at the John F. Kennedy Presidential Library, https://www.jfklibrary.org/learn/about-jfk/the-kennedy-family/robert-f-kennedy/robert-f-kennedy-speeches/remarks-to-the-cleveland-city-club-april-5-1968.

10. Danilo Dolci, quoted in Joseph Geraci, "Danilo Dolci: The Gandhi of Sicily," Satyagraha Foundation for Nonviolence Studies, March 22, 2013, https://www.satyagrahafoundation.org/danilo-dolci-the-gandhi-of-sicily/.

11. Susan Jacoby, *Wild Justice: The Evolution of Revenge* (New York: Harper & Row, 1983), chapter 6.

12. Shantideva, *The Way of the Bodhisattva,* trans. Padmakara Translation Group (Boston: Shambhala Publications, 2006), 48–49.

13. Bhikkhu Nanamoli and Bhikkhu Bodhi, trans. *The Middle Length Discourses of the Buddha: A Translation of the Majjhima Nikaya* (Somerville, MA: Wisdom Publications, 1995), 223.

14. Geshe Langri Thangpa, "Eight Verses of Training the Mind," rev. 2012, Lotsawa House, https://www.lotsawahouse.org/tibetan-masters/geshe-langri-thangpa/eight-verses-training-mind.

15. St. Ignatius, "Epistle to the Romans," trans. Alexander Roberts and James Donaldson, in *Ante-Nicene Fathers,* vol. 1, ed. Alexander Roberts, James Donaldson, and A. Cleveland Coxe

(Buffalo, NY: Christian Literature Publishing Co., 1885), revised and edited for *New Advent* by Kevin Knight, www .newadvent.org/fathers/0107.htm.

16. William Shakespeare, *Troilus and Cressida*, act 3, scene 2.

17. Martin Luther King Jr., "The Quest for Peace and Justice" (Nobel lecture, Oslo, Norway, December 11, 1964), https:// www.nobelprize.org/prizes/peace/1964/king/lecture/.

ABOUT THE AUTHOR

DAVID RICHO, PHD, is a psychotherapist, writer, and workshop leader. He has taught at a variety of places, including Esalen, Spirit Rock Buddhist Retreat Center, San Francisco Zen Center, and San Damiano Retreat Center. He shares his time between Santa Barbara and San Francisco, California. His website is davericho.com.

In recent years, David has been giving talks and workshops on alternatives to retaliation in relationships and in society. In this work he has greatly appreciated being joined by four wise and respected colleagues: Shosan Victoria Austin and Barry Brown in the Bay Area and Radhule Weininger and Michael Kearney in Santa Barbara.

BOOKS

Being True to Life: Poetic Paths to Personal Growth (Shambhala, 2009)

By Your Side: How to Find Soulful Allies and Become One to Others (Shambhala, 2024)

Coming Home to Who You Are: Discovering Your Natural Capacity for Love, Integrity, and Compassion (Shambhala, 2011)

Daring to Trust: Opening Ourselves to Real Love and Intimacy
(Shambhala, 2010)

Everyday Commitments: Choosing a Life of Love, Realism, and Acceptance (Shambhala, 2007)

Everything Ablaze: Meditating on the Mystical Vision of Teilhard de Chardin (Paulist Press, 2017)

The Five Longings: What We've Always Wanted and Already Have (Shambhala, 2017)

The Five Things We Cannot Change and the Happiness We Find by Embracing Them (Shambhala, 2005)

Five True Things: A Little Guide to Embracing Life's Big Challenges (Shambhala, 2019)

How to Be an Adult: A Handbook on Psychological and Spiritual Integration (Paulist Press, 1991)

How to Be an Adult in Faith and Spirituality (Paulist Press, 2011)

How to Be an Adult in Love: Letting Love in Safely and Showing It Recklessly (Shambhala, 2013)

How to Be an Adult in Relationships: The Five Keys to Mindful Loving (Shambhala, 2002, rev. ed. 2021)

The Power of Coincidence: How Life Shows Us What We Need to Know (Shambhala, 2007)

The Power of Grace: Recognizing Unexpected Gifts on the Path (Shambhala, 2014)

Ready: How to Know When to Go and When to Stay (Shambhala, 2022)

The Sacred Heart of the World: Restoring Mystical Devotion to Our Spiritual Life (Paulist Press, 2007)

Shadow Dance: Liberating the Power and Creativity of Your Dark Side (Shambhala, 1999)

To Thine Own Self Be True: Shakespeare as Therapist and Spiritual Guide (Paulist Press, 2023)

Triggers: How We Can Stop Reacting and Start Healing (Shambhala, 2019)

When Catholic Means Cosmic: Opening to a Big-Hearted Faith (Paulist Press, 2015)

When Love Meets Fear: How to Become Defense-less and Resource-full (Paulist Press, 1997)

When Mary Becomes Cosmic: A Jungian and Mystical Path to the Divine Feminine (Paulist Press, 2016)

When the Past Is Present: Healing the Emotional Wounds That Sabotage Our Relationships (Shambhala, 2008)

Wholeness and Holiness: How to Be Sane, Spiritual, and Saintly (Orbis, 2020)

You Are Not What You Think: The Egoless Path to Self-Esteem and Generous Love (Shambhala, 2015)

01 14